Praise for *Personal Heart Power*

"This book is outstanding! The crystalline clarity in which Grace Lynn and Michelle Marie masterfully guide us with practices to embody our *Personal Heart Power* is to be celebrated! I, personally, have been enriched by implementing the heart-based practices to maintain an optimally balanced, love-infused life."

— Shelley Darling
    Author of *Songline of the Heart*
    Founder of *Evolutionary Dowsing*, and *Good of the Whole*

"During a time in history where fear is prevalent on television and in the news, Michelle and Grace excel at teaching you how to be present and transition from operating from a mode of fear into one of love. When employing the Personal Heart Power Tools, you'll realize your own power to choose love and interact with a calm mind. Taking control of your personal heart power has an effect not only on you but on your friends, your community, and the entire world."

— Kathleen Brooks
    New York Times, Wall Street Journal & USA Today
    Bestselling Author

"*Personal Heart Power* is a beautiful catalyst for anyone looking to find more love, happiness, and meaning in their lives. This brave and powerful book thoughtfully guides readers on a journey of self-exploration and positively connects us to ourselves and each other. This is the true path to peace."

— Julie Burton
    Author of *The Self-Care Solution—A Modern Mother's Must Have Guide to Health and Well-Being*
    Founder of *Modern Well*

"I wish I had this book as a young psychotherapist! *Personal Heart Power* is a brilliant guide for navigating troubling times of great transformation. This book is necessary reading for all stages of life and sets us up to be more loving, kind, compassionate, inclusive, and free. What a gift and treasure!"

—Julie Krull, PhD
Award-winning author of *Fractured Grace*
Host of *The Dr. Julie Show: All Things Connected*
President and founder of *Good of the Whole*

"In a world where so many feel overwhelmed, the authors of *Personal Heart Power* guide the reader on a journey where elevated consciousness leads to better choices, more loving outcomes, and the relief from fear."

— Annie Griffiths
Founder of *Ripple Effect Images*
Photographer for *National Geographic*

"Grace Lynn and Michelle Marie have created this brilliant guide to support us in making the shift from fear to love. *Personal Heart Power* is filled with both a clear map and practical guidance to navigate us during this powerful transformation."

— Julie Daley, CPCC
Innovation Catalyst, Transformational Leadership Coach

"*Personal Heart Power* provides a compelling framework to guide heart-mind-spirit connection. The content, stories, and practical tools inspire intentional living and making choices from the Mode of Love. Three cheers for the love that emerges."

— Deb Sakry Lande
Co-author of *Universal Intentions*

"I applaud the enduring effort and dedication of the spiritually gifted Michelle Marie and Grace Lynn, who encourage humanity to up-level beyond fear to love. They offer us a path through the dense labyrinth of the heart, and a guide to developing our own personal power using the domain of love."

— Joan Solomon
Artist
Author of *Spirits in the Garden*

"There are many ways through the chaos of this life, but the heart is the keeper of the evolutionary path. I know that to be true, but how do you embody the heart's directives? The authors of this book have created an invitation and structure to both understand and follow your heart's path, moving you to claim more and more of who you are so you can engage the world from a place of love: for self and others."

— Joan Steffend
Author of *peace in peace out*, and *...and she sparkled*
Speaker, listener, former HGTV host, and professional wonderer

"This wise, insightful book will give you deep insights as well as practical steps to help you grow in every aspect of your life; especially in relation to yourself and those you love."

— Heather McElhatton
Host of *A Beautiful World*
Author of *Pretty Little Mistakes*

"Michelle and Grace have written an essential book that provides a clear template for living from the heart. *Personal Heart Power* is inspiring, uplifting and, mostly, it is an important read for anyone who seeks to shift from the operating system of fear into the sovereign state of love. The content has the potential to be life-changing."

— Marin Bach-Antonson
Magdalene Rose Priestess

Personal
HEART
POWER

TRANSFORMING TO A LOVE-FOCUSED LIFE

For Jennifer,

With the Power of Love,
Michelle

MICHELLE MARIE
& GRACE LYNN

Capucia LLC
211 Pauline Drive #513
York, PA 17402
www.capuciapublishing.com
Send questions to: support@capuciapublishing.com

Paperback ISBN: 978-1-954920-43-9
eBook ISBN: 978-1-954920-44-6
Library of Congress Control Number: 2022918108

Cover Design: Ranilo Cabo
Layout: Ranilo Cabo
Editor and Proofreader: Simon Whaley
Book Midwife: Karen Everitt

Printed in the United States of America

Capucia LLC is proud to be a part of the Tree Neutral® program. Tree Neutral offsets the number of trees consumed in the production and printing of this book by taking proactive steps such as planting trees in direct proportion to the number of trees used to print books. To learn more about Tree Neutral, please visit treeneutral.com.

This book is dedicated to everyone searching for their Personal Heart Power so they may create the love-focused life they desire.

Authors' Note

We suggest reading this book all the way through the first time to get a comprehensive understanding of what *Personal Heart Power* is and what it can do for you. It is important to read at a pace that allows you to understand the concepts and optimize your personal growth. We have organized the book into three sections. If you are a reader who prefers a framework before the process, then read the sections in the order presented. If you are a process-before-framework reader, then read Section 2 first, followed by Section 1. Section 3 is best read last.

Allow yourself to absorb what we've presented and make it fun. As you come to apply these concepts and use the tools we've identified to help you on your Personal Heart Journey, you may find it useful to re-read chapters at a time that is relevant for you.

And although we are here to guide you along your journey, sharing your experience with other readers may create another layer of support. This could be through:

- your book club,
- a like-minded friend,
- your partner,
- a counselor, or coach,
- additional support from our websites:
    - lovevoicerising.com
    - globalheartteam.org

However you choose to read this book, we're delighted to be part of your Personal Heart Journey.

Contents

FEAR TO LOVE

PERSONAL HEART POWER TOOLBOX

Personal

Heart

Introduction

Hello! Welcome to your *Personal Heart Power Journey! This is your first amazing step towards discovering a new way of being that supports your inner desires. *Personal Heart Power* will show you:

- how to let go of the fears that have kept you stuck in a fear-focused life,
- how to look for ways to feel more love in your life,
- and how to gain the power you need to create a more love-focused life.

We are excited you have decided to immerse yourself into a deeper discovery of who you are and why you are here. To do this, you will need to get to know your *Personal Heart.

Throughout this book, you will see words with an asterisk (*) in front of them. In fact, you've already seen a few of them. This means this is the first mention of a word or phrase that appears in our glossary. We will, of course, explain these words or phrases as we delve deeper into the subject with you, but if you come across a phrase and want to know what it means, then the glossary will be the quickest way to inform yourself. Familiarizing yourself with the terminology will help you create a deeper connection to your Personal Heart Power Journey.

Many of us long for our *Personal Heart Power, but few of us are willing to acknowledge and take the time to pursue it. So, by showing up here, you are already demonstrating you have the courage and readiness for this journey.

This book focuses on opening your Personal Heart and connecting it to your calm mind. A calm mind is different from an empty mind. It can still be full of thoughts, but it is not chaotic and stressful. A calm mind is peaceful and discerning.

If the idea of having a calm mind is unfamiliar or challenging for you, some resources that might be beneficial are *The Power of Now* by Eckhart Tolle,[1] *Aware: The Science and Practice of Presence* by Dr. Daniel Siegel, MD,[2] *The Miracle of Mindfulness* by Thich Nhat Hanh,[3] *Wired for Joy* by Laurel Mellin, PhD,[4] and *Positive Intelligence* by Shirzad Chamine.[5]

If you find yourself with high levels of stress in your mind, consider seeking support from one of these or other resources. It's important we find the mental tranquility we need to allow ourselves to discover and connect to our Personal Heart Power.

Being led by fear or love in our decision-making process determines whether we are surviving or thriving in life. The choice is ours. Our goal is to present you with ways that allow you to create a life you thrive in. There is no judgment here as you follow your own unique path. The road we have chosen may differ from the one you are meant to travel. It is both our uniqueness and our similarities in the journey that bind us to an interconnected world. The choices each of us make influences how the world operates collectively. The excitement of knowing we have the power to influence the reality we live in can be inspiring.

We'll help you voyage deep into your Personal Heart so you can realize how your thoughts, feelings, and behaviors are creating your life. We'll show you how learning to live from love allows fear to become your valuable informant, rather than a life-crippling detrimental force. As you gain understanding and use the tools we offer here, you can become the leader of your life! You will know *your* Personal Heart Power and recognize how the choices you make will either extinguish or ignite your power.

Before you begin this journey with us, we want you to understand us, your navigators, and why we are cheering you on as you discover your Personal Heart Power. We are Grace Lynn and Michelle Marie. We met at a Barbara Marx Hubbard retreat in Taos, New Mexico, in September 2016. Grace had already started her *Loving Journey* program and was expanding the Global Heart Team, a group of people dedicated to sharing love with humanity and the world. Michelle was immersed in philanthropic endeavors and had recently wrapped up a capital campaign for affordable housing. We were both following a deeper calling—a calling from our Personal Hearts. We didn't know it, but we were beginning a journey to recognize the potential of our Personal Heart Power.

We connected on a break, which led to a walk. On that simple stroll, we quickly found we were united in our favorite theme in life: Unconditional Love.

After the retreat, we reconnected through a mutual friend who believed we would be a good match to create a one-day workshop for a retreat in Taos, New Mexico, in the fall of 2017. Little did we know then that our presentation, the *Love Bridge Between Fear and Love*, would reveal a soul-sister relationship that would lead us to co-create a six-week teleseminar called *A New Way of Loving* in the spring of 2018. With the success of the teleseminar, we felt we had more to create together. *Personal Heart Power* is the result of following our hearts.

Before our lives journeyed together, we had both experienced a *conscious awareness of the opportunity to seek our Personal Heart Powers. We each had been through many moments when we'd had enough. Enough courage, pain, desire, success, failure, encouragement… so many *enoughs* that we were able to recognize that our choices were points of *transition. We could make choices that either connected us to the *Source of Unconditional Love or not. In this book, the **Source of Unconditional Love is the origin of the *energy that fuels our Personal Heart with Unconditional Love.**

We recognized that it is when we are truly aware of the choices available to us that we can consider which option allows us to open our heart to further our Personal Heart Journey.

Our conscious awareness of all the thoughts, feelings, and behaviors… the aha moments, the confusion, the joy… has allowed us to work together toward our shared desire to tap into our Personal Heart Power. This has led us to the same collaborative home.

As you read a glimpse into our Personal Heart stories, be mindful that they may trigger some challenging memories with feelings in relation to your story. Take the time to reflect and feel what is rising within you. It will be valuable information for your journey to a more love-focused life.

Grace's Personal Heart Journey

Like all Personal Heart Journeys, my journey began the day I was born. My grandmother told me the story about my first day of life. She reminded me almost every year on my birthday, for thirty-two years, how I ruined my aunt's wedding because my mother went into labor early that October morning. My father drove my mother to the hospital, which meant he couldn't walk his younger sister down the aisle on her wedding day.

My grandmother would then share how I put my mom through eighteen hours of hard labor because I was struggling in the birth canal, only for the doctor to use forceps to pull me out. When my grandmother saw me for the first time, she would describe my face as being so crooked from the forceps delivery that she cried so hard she couldn't drive home and had to call a taxi to take her home.

Further disappointment added to the story. I was supposed to be a son. In the early 1960s, in an Irish Catholic family, my father, like other fathers of the day, preferred having a boy first—especially because one of their duties was to carry the family name to the next generation. So, on the first day of my life, I disappointed four major people in my family. I soon learned that I hated feeling not good enough, being judged by others, and sensing others' disappointment in me.

Many early memories from childhood were fueled with fear: fear of doing the wrong thing, which could lead to punishments ranging from verbal judgments and loud warnings to physical reinforcement with a hand, belt, or whatever was within reach at the time. I learned quickly that I received more positive attention if I were a *good girl* and pleased people. I grew up living in survival mode, as modeled by my parents.

I do remember some happy times, like swimming in our backyard pool with my three younger sisters and friends, going to the state fair with my family, and family vacations to Florida. Now, I can fully appreciate that my parents loved me the best they could and took care of me with the skills they had learned from their parents and the cultural beliefs at the time.

One of my earliest conscious memories was when I was around four years old and watching a Miss America Pageant with my parents. I decided to put on my pink pajamas with the frilly ruffles around the collar and bottom edge. Prancing around the living room pretending to be a Miss America contestant, I felt happy.

"Could I be Miss America when I grow up?" I asked my father.

"No," he stated in a matter-of-fact tone.

That two-letter word drove me to my bedroom crying so hard that when my mom came in to check on me, she thought I had the measles. I blamed my crooked eyes, cheeks, and ears for why I couldn't become Miss America, unaware of the fact that the probability of being Miss America is very slim for any girl. With my hands, I tried pushing and forcing my crooked face back to being level to look like other pretty girls. I spent what felt like hours trying to correct my facial lopsidedness, only to give up feeling ugly, rejected, and hating my face even more because I couldn't be Miss America someday. That was the conscious beginning of my self-hate loop for my body and especially my crooked face.

I filled my teen years by overcompensating with high achievements in middle school and high school academics and extracurricular activities. I thought high achievements would compensate for being not good enough, not pretty enough, not lovable, and not worthy. No matter how successful I was, it never felt good enough to please my inner critic, who was in full authority over what I thought about myself and others.

My college years were intense, trying to be smart enough to get into a physical therapy program. Even once I'd made it, it was still challenging to keep up being *as smart* as others and keep my fear of failure at bay. However, I graduated with a Bachelor in Health Science in physical therapy. After graduating, I immediately started graduate school in education while working full time as a physical therapist. My drive to overachieve was in full gear to overcompensate and suppress my stressful beliefs that I was not good enough.

During the summer before my sophomore year of college, I dated a guy whom I'd known since high school. Six months later, on New Year's Eve, we fought about who he wanted to be with on New Year's Eve. He chose his male friends over me, and I never heard from him again.

Emotional pain from that abandonment further reinforced my stressful beliefs: *I am not pretty enough, not good enough, not worthy of love,* and most of all, *I am not lovable.* This deep hurt of rejection sealed my heart so tightly that I thought I would never open my heart again.

During my last semester in physical therapy school, however, I met a geology graduate student who rocked my whole fear-focused life. He showered me with Unconditional Love and modeled for me a love-focused relationship.

Slowly and over time, I trusted his love, to the point of being so vulnerable that I opened my Personal Heart to take in his love and give him love in return. We got married and had two children, creating the life we wanted while sharing this Unconditional Love the best we could with our beautiful children—by no means perfectly. Believe me, we made many mistakes as parents along the way. But then our world changed forever.

On August 30, 1997, the same day Princess Diana died, my sister's family—herself, her husband, their three-year-old daughter, and eighteen-month-old son—were in a car accident. My sister slipped into a coma and her husband died that day. Luckily, the two children in the back seat survived unharmed.

Within an hour of hearing the tragic news, I boarded an airplane and landed at the closest airport to the regional hospital, where my sister was being treated. That night, I talked to the social worker regarding my niece and nephew. I called my husband. We agreed we would take our niece and nephew in as long as necessary until she recovered enough to raise her children. Overnight, we went from having a six-year-old daughter and four-year-old son to four children in our family. Two weeks later, the physical therapy company where I worked went bankrupt and stole the money from my 401(k) plan.

In a moment, my life flipped upside down—very little was the same. Financial stress from losing my job and fearful thoughts about whether my sister would ever recover created many worries resulting from this stressful situation. I worried if I could be a good enough mother to her children and if we would have enough money. These constant stressful thoughts helped me to avoid feeling the deeper sadness of my sister being in a coma and feeling guilty for being her children's mother. This unfolding journey had many challenges and opportunities for personal growth for the next twenty-three years until she passed.

My personal spiritual journey was inspired by the desire to heal my sister. It started by learning different healing techniques with the hope of healing her back to being normal. However, nothing significantly seemed to change her minimally conscious status.

While learning these healing practices, I slowly began healing myself. I began forgiving myself for not being perfect, for my face and body not being perfect, for not being good enough, and I began to love myself unconditionally. With each higher vibrational choice I made, I looked at myself differently, through the eyes of compassion rather than judgment.

Over the years, loving myself and others became easier. Life became easier as I focused on getting myself in better balance on all levels. Having less stress in my life created more capacity to feel more Unconditional Love, forgiveness, acceptance, and compassion for myself and others. I explored my personal growth: one workshop, one retreat, one group, one counseling session, and one book at a time. Two of my spiritual mentors, Sr. Marcia Jehn and Jeremy Taylor DMin., blessed me with their wisdom and loving presence in my life.

Over the years, I have learned and practiced many different tools to process effectively through my painful feelings from childhood and adulthood. I still use some of these tools in my life to maintain balance in the aspects of my Personal Heart. My family and friends have also benefited from me being more loving and in balance more of the time. My Personal Heart journey continues to be a daily practice of higher vibrational thoughts, feelings, and behaviors more of the time, and I am grateful to be thriving in a love-focused life.

Michelle's Personal Heart Journey

Like anyone else, I have a myriad of stories—ranging from incredibly painful to great joy—that form my life. These stories inform the choices I make and they have accumulated to produce my Personal Heart Power Story.

The night my mom's water broke, she was home alone. There was no car, no phone, and no husband to assist her at that moment. She did not panic as she determined what to do while she waited for my dad to return, hoping it would be soon. She believed it would be OK. She calmly chose to lie down and wait. Dad returned home shortly, and they made their way to the hospital, just in time.

I was rapidly entering the world with the umbilical cord wrapped around my neck. Urgently, the doctor told my mom to quit pushing, which she wasn't doing; I was simply ready to be born. Although my mom remembers the turmoil, she trusted the doctor to take care of things, and he did. Soon, she was overjoyed to be holding me. My dad felt relieved and ecstatic when he heard the news. I was born fully attached to the love and calm of my mother. She chose not to panic and went with the flow. That's what I was born into. I believe we enter this world connected to the Source of Unconditional Love, and I was born into a home of love. This combination formed my foundation.

My parents named me Michelle Marie. In third grade, they gave me a bookmark with my name, Michelle, and its meaning: godly woman. I ingested the meaning and felt joy and a powerful responsibility to be a godly woman. As one might imagine, there were pros and cons to that.

In my family, I could dance to the beat of my drum. I felt comfortable being who I was. They may not have always appreciated my drumbeat, but I never felt like they expected me to be someone other than who I was. This gave me a naïve resilience for years to come.

I do not remember a self-conscious moment until I was entering the fourth grade, and I had to switch schools. I walked in as the stranger, *the other*, to an established classroom of children. I did not understand then that *the other* can be negative. This is often a brutal turning point for people, but I carried on believing this was an exciting new adventure.

We had a math bee early in the school year. It got down to me and another girl. Everyone was rooting for her except for the one person who transferred schools with me. The other girl won, but rather than seeing myself as a loser, I saw myself in second place in the whole class!

My innocent view of the world also served me well when I was nicknamed Alpo that same year. Although Alpo was a popular dog food brand, I did not see it as them calling me a dog. Alpo was being advertised as the best dog food for your dog. In my mind, everyone loved their dogs, and therefore, my new classmates loved me. Naïve, I know, but to this day I believe it was because I did not take it personally that I was, eventually, able to fit into my new school and develop friendships.

I switched schools again in sixth grade, and harsh realities presented themselves. I was told by a girl that I had to choose which friend group I wanted to be a part of. I could not figure out why there had to be a choice, but it became clear I had to choose. I could no longer hang out in two different groups. I chose the other group. That was the beginning of separation and abandonment for me. The beat of my drum started to fade. In that choice, I began pushing down and silencing parts of myself, even as other parts flourished.

Since then, even as I thrived, I have often felt this world was trying to make me choose, silence me, invalidate me, and make me something different from my authentic self. This made it challenging to maintain the beat of my drum.

With each passing year, the beat of my drum faded. Eventually, it was replaced by society's drum, and I fell more into step with the rhythm of society's expectations. I learned that pleasing other people gave me rewards. I began to believe this was the way of a godly woman. Sacrificing what would be better for me for what would be better for someone else became an integral part of my being.

For many years, I felt like I was the only one who had to hide parts of herself. The people who seemed the most like me seemed genuinely happy marching to the beat of society's drum. People who did not seem happy seemed so angry. I found ways to be happy. My drumbeat faded. When the burden of the paradigm beat became too confusing or painful, I would escape to the comforting bliss of my connection to the Source of Unconditional Love—the keeper of my stowed away drum.

Surprisingly, my greatest struggle has not been seeking a connection with the Source of Unconditional Love, but rather my connection with the human experience. It wasn't until I was well into my forties that I realized this! At my core, I believed most people were rooted in love, and that fear rose as an exception, not as an option in which to base your life. I believed the world was good, whole, and loving. I still do. I still struggle to acknowledge that most people operate from the *Mode of Fear more frequently than they do from the *Mode of Love. It is challenging to connect to the humanness.

The summer after I graduated high school, my dad, who was a member of the Jaycees, asked me to run in the pageant they sponsored for Miss Thief River Falls. That thought had never crossed my mind. By this time, I had incorporated many *not-good-enough* thoughts into my way of being. I thought I did not have talent. I was too fat for the swimsuit part, and I certainly was not as pretty as anyone else who would run. The world had written upon my soul, yet, my rock, my idol, the person who most supported me, believed I could do this, and he said it would mean a lot to him.

I wanted to believe my dad. I trusted him and I wanted to please him. So, I ran for Miss Thief River Falls. In reflection, we were both right. He was right for believing in me, and I was right for trusting him. I did not win the pageant, but I learned I was talented enough, thin enough, and pretty enough to have one of the most important people in my life believe in me. I had won a victory for me and my dad. Bonus: no one booed or laughed me off the stage.

It was one of the last encouragingly supportive experiences so tightly connected to my dad. As I began my journey out on my own, my dad began his journey as an alcoholic—an incredibly painful paradigm shift from which we never fully recovered.

Although we remained close, some demons won that battle. Fear of abandonment infiltrated my human existence. The deafening beat of the societal drum and the shifted relationship with my dad had silenced my drum. I dealt with that by abandoning myself. Of course, I did not realize this until I had my son, but I am getting ahead of myself.

At the time I married, my husband and I were two independent people who loved each other. However, we struggled to learn how to navigate marriage in relation to society's expectations. Soon, I barely remembered I had a drum. Even when I would escape, to connect with the Source of Unconditional Love, it wasn't to play my drum; it was to be held by the Spirit of this Love for the removal of the deep pain of life. I could not believe how cruel this world was; perhaps even worse was that I was so naïve to it. I was in my own silent struggles and did not yet know it.

As the years unfolded, the pain increased and the abandonment of myself was commonplace. My way out of my turmoil, and as a way of survival, was that I remained connected to the Source of Unconditional Love. This connection began making it more challenging to remain connected to my humanity. I knew I needed to be connected to both. It took me years to rise like a phoenix from my ashes, but rise I did.

I believed I was enough, but I could see the world wanted more from me. I heard the beat: more, more, more… and more I gave. I gave abundantly, exhaustively, numbly, absently, and with a smile on my face. I was no longer going with the flow and love I was born into.

Until one day, when I was blessed with complete clarity that I could no longer exist in that way. It was the day I learned I was pregnant. I reconnected to my life's purpose. In that instant, literally, I had complete clarity that my purpose was to live out loud as my authentic self. It was time to rise!

I searched for my drum and began to play. Secretly at first, then quietly, then slowly but surely, I could hear the beat of my drum… I could feel my beat… then I could dance to my beat. I wish I could say it happened in an instant, but it took years and a commanding intention to reclaim my sovereignty, to be conscious of my life, and to choose to operate with my Personal Heart Power.

I still struggle, but I struggle in a healthy way, and I thrive. I live with a loving relationship between my Personal Heart and mind in union with Unconditional Love—a beacon of light that is easy to find, especially in my darkest days. Each journey I took through the dark night of my soul allowed me to reclaim another piece of my sovereignty. Once I realized that experiencing the pain of the darkness is what would transform that pain into a more expanded experience of Unconditional Love in my human existence, it became easier to say, "Yes!" to the transition. It is fun to dance to the beat of my drum.

I bow humbly in gratitude for an extraordinary existence and for the path that I have chosen for my Personal Heart Power journey. Despite the pains and struggles, it has offered me much joy in life. Adding to that joy and my drumbeat are the various educational, professional, and philanthropic opportunities I have experienced. I genuinely love to learn and consider it a wasted day if I have not learned something new. I also thoroughly appreciate working with, learning from, and inspiring people. This is what fills me up the most!

Everything I have experienced has prepared me to help write this book and establish *Love Voice Rising* (www.lovevoicerising.com) with the desire to guide others to step into the life of their fullest potential by living from their Personal Heart Power! I know now that my connection to the Source of Unconditional Love is my greatest Personal Heart Power. I also know that many are struggling, dancing to the beat of society's drum of expectations. That is why Grace and I have written this book. We know how our stories, our journeys, and the pages that follow may benefit others who are yearning for connection. If you can relate to this, then dust off your drum in readiness to reconnect to your beat and discover your Personal Heart Power!

♥ ♥ ♥

We both have many stories of great challenges and great joys. We recognize how each of them has been moments of grace to connect more deeply and gratefully to the Source of Unconditional Love. The stupidity, failures, mistakes, and feelings of *not enough* have been as powerful—if not more powerful—than all the successful moments for shifting our Personal Hearts to a more love-focused life.

We both now know that when we have a choice to make, we have the greatest opportunity to influence our own lives by consciously using the wisdom gained from experiences to make a decision. We have learned through experience that when we operate from and for love, our lives are more fulfilling. Our thoughts, feelings, and behaviors have become our messengers into how our life is working at any given moment. When we feel the anger, frustration, and irritation of life, we feel empowered to do our Personal Heart work—no matter how challenging—so we can rebalance with the feelings of joy, happiness, and peace.

Together, we have collaborated to unite our experiences, education, knowledge, and desires to create this book. We have filled it with foundational information, Personal Heart stories, Personal Heart Power Tools, and—most of all—*Unconditional Love to carry you through to use your Personal Heart Power!

As you empower yourself, you will have opportunities to create the life you desire rooted in love. This will not always be easy, but with each step you take towards a deeper connection to your authentic self, you will gain greater awareness of your power to choose between a life operating from fear or a life operating from love. We'll show you how to choose love. Let the journey begin!

CHAPTER 1

Committing to Your Personal Heart Power Journey

I magine driving down a winding road that carries you to your wonderful dream home near the ocean. It is a perfectly sunny day. A sense of joyfulness envelops you at the thought of living in your dream home. As you pull in, you notice the quaint beach cottage embraced by the beauty of the front gardens, full of flowers and luscious green landscaping of varying textures and hues. Your smile broadens to a grin as you appreciate the care the outdoor spaces have been given.

Walking around your home, you're enthralled by the breathtaking view of the ocean with its white, silky, sandy beach and the gentle lapping of the waves. The sense of peace and contentment is intoxicating. At this moment, you turn and notice the beauty and strength of the home itself. It is built high upon four strong, solid pillars to keep it safe from the changing tides. You have the courage to enter because you feel a sense of arriving home. Deep down in your heart, it feels safe and welcoming.

In the same way that we journey to find our dream home, we also go on a journey to find our Personal Heart. Our Personal Heart is the sensory center for our collective energetic experiences of thoughts, feelings, and behaviors. These collective experiences are influenced by two primary vibrational energies: the Mode of Fear and the Mode of Love. With no direct action from ourselves, these Modes unconsciously influence the choices we make in our lives—choices that are not always beneficial for us. How many times have we stopped and wished, in hindsight, that we'd made a different choice? And with our regret, we believe a different choice would have made our life happier than we are now.

The good news is that we can change this. Once we understand how our Personal Heart is the home of our life, we can then take steps to look after it and make conscious decisions that will give us the life we dream about. Even with a history of poor choices, we do not have to live a life with regret. Rather, it is about gathering wisdom from our mistakes to create a love-focused life.

If you are curious to discover what your home is currently like, tap into your courage and go inside—inside your Personal Heart. As you stand there, inside your Personal Heart of today, consider how much sunlight is filtering in. Is it dark, moody, and fearful? Or is it overflowing with beautiful, golden sunshine, flooding love into every corner? Or perhaps something in between.

The level of sunlight represents the amount of fear or love filtering into our Personal Heart home. This influences how we think, feel, and behave. If we want to flood this home with more sunlight, then it's time to go on a journey of awareness.

This journey will map the discovery of our Personal Heart Power. We begin this conscious journey because we are yearning for something in our life to be different. Our stories in the introduction are examples of this yearning. We want to explore and change the way we function in our Personal Heart. Such willingness to be open to learning and shifting to new ways of being helps us arrive at our destination: our Personal Heart Power.

We've used a dream home analogy to help you visualize your Personal Heart Power. Many of us know what our dream home is like. Here, it is a beach home, but feel free to create your own. This book is your glorious road trip to your dream home!

Once we are aware of our Personal Heart, it gives us the potential to build a deeper, healthier, and more loving relationship with ourselves. This awareness determines what we perceive, the choices we believe we have, and how we will live in the world.

Our Personal Heart influences our thoughts, feelings, and behaviors. Learning to build a more familiar relationship with these three experiences encourages us to become the author of our life, instead of being a victim, or always *reacting* to life. When we choose to know our heart deeply, it becomes our compass, determining which direction we want to go with each step of our life. In fact, our Personal Heart determines how we navigate through our life, whether or not we are aware of it. The good news is, with more awareness, we will consciously recognize more choices in our life.

Once we decide to be conscious of our Personal Heart, we then get to choose what we hold on to and what we let go of. To begin with, it may be difficult to believe we have this much ownership of how we feel every day, but it truly is our choice. If we make choices rooted in love more often, we will transition from the Mode of Fear to the Mode of Love. This will root our Personal Heart in Unconditional Love, and we will transform as we use our Personal Heart Power.

In the same way that we fall in love with our dream home, we want you to fall in love with the energetic connection that is Unconditional Love. **Unconditional Love is loving energy without expectations.**

It supports, encourages, motivates, and empathizes with us. Conditional or personal love creates rules that dictate whether love will be given out from or taken into our Personal Heart. This book will help you explore new ways of operating in your heart. You will learn how to live more consciously and effectively. This helps you build your bridge to your Personal Heart Power using Unconditional Love.

Personal Heart Power is the ability to operate from the Mode of Love within our Personal Heart while interacting optimally with a calm mind. A magical connection occurs when we have a calm mind supporting our heart's desire. This connection creates a loving union that energizes our soul's purpose. With awareness and practical tools, we can create the life we want to have rooted in Unconditional Love. This union, between our calm mind and open Personal Heart, is our Personal Heart Power.

As we show you how to go inside your Personal Heart, you will discover your current relationship and connection with the Source of Unconditional Love. Some people call this source God, Allah, Buddha, Source, The Universe, Spirit, or Gaia. You may even have another name for it.

The particular name is not the priority. The priority is the opportunity to feel connected to this Source of Unconditional Love inside our Personal Heart, which is available to anyone. It is our conscious awareness in any moment that allows us to feel this connection to Unconditional Love in our Personal Heart.

We believe that becoming self-aware of our Personal Heart is the most empowering journey we can take.

We are not saying life will be easy just because we gain a greater awareness of our Personal Heart. However, anything that increases our quality of life is worth the effort. Adding Unconditional Love and releasing crippling fears are worthwhile for all of us. We get to decide how far we can grow.

Think of something you want to change in your life. Now imagine having the ability to make that happen—to create in your life what you desire. Imagine having the capability and energy to manifest what you need to bring your desire to fruition.

This can occur when we connect to our Personal Heart. This loving connection is the glue between the calm mind and our open Personal Heart. When we achieve this unification, our Personal Heart Power is ignited.

Therefore, to know our Personal Heart, we must raise our awareness of it and bring it into our consciousness. For it is when we make conscious decisions that we can bring about the changes we truly desire. **Conscious Awareness is our ability to recognize the information we have in the present moment.** With conscious awareness, we become aware of our choices and their potential outcomes. This awareness allows us to make the choices to manifest our heart's desire! Are you ready to put the time and effort into knowing your Personal Heart?

Throughout this process, it's important to be gentle and kind to yourself rather than critical and judgmental. You may discover some deeper beliefs and truths that you have not been aware of before. Some of these may make you feel excited and empowered. Others may be painful and challenging to recognize in yourself. Find your courage to go through the entire process without judgment. In the end, you will have a deeper understanding and compassion for who you are and a connection to your Personal Heart Power.

There are many paths to connect you with what we are calling the Personal Heart. This book shares our path. Our intention is not only to connect you to your Personal Heart, but also to show you how to empower it to work in sync with your calm mind. This will help you be more effective in creating the life you desire.

This is our model—a framework to connect the calm mind with an open Personal Heart to help you achieve a more conscious way of living. Ultimately, we hope our model helps you find the path that empowers and enlightens you to live to your fullest potential.

We have both been on our Personal Heart journeys and gathered our experiences to create a user-friendly process that will support you on your journey to connect more intimately to your Personal Heart Power. We do this because we know that all people who consciously connect to their Personal Heart Power enhance our world. And when all these Personal Hearts act as one, it creates a love-focused *Global Heart. Imagine a world whose Global Heart is rooted in love rather than fear.

Today, the Global Heart, powered by the energies of each person's heart, struggles to connect to the power of Unconditional Love. Most people contribute fear energy to our Global Heart. The best way to live in a more loving world is to begin with your own Personal Heart.

It's the transformation of our Personal Heart from a heart full of fear to one full of love that leads us to our Personal Heart Power. This power, rooted in Unconditional Love, contributes Unconditional Love to the Global Heart. When enough individuals choose to shift their Personal Heart from Fear to Unconditional Love, the same will happen for the Global Heart.

That's why we are delighted you want to explore this journey with us. We have connected to our Personal Heart Power, rooted in Unconditional Love, and we are grateful that you are about to do the same. These Personal Heart connections are making our world more loving!

Remember, this is a time to spend in self-reflection without judgment and with compassion for yourself. Focus on truth, honesty, vulnerability, integrity, and self-care. When you set an intention of what Personal Heart growth you would like to experience, you will facilitate the change you are hoping to see. Choices, rooted in love, will imprint new ways of functioning for you in your Personal Heart.

Imagine being able to process your thoughts and feelings in a way that creates healthy behaviors which lead you to feel more joy, abundance, peace, and love. By becoming infused with this new loving way of operating in the world, you will also shine more loving light on those around you and in the world in which you live.

As we give you more information, Personal Heart Power Tools, and a greater understanding of your Personal Heart, you will have the ability to show your Personal Heart Power in a loving way for yourself and others.

You are embarking on a journey to Unconditional Love. Take this moment to commit, with intention, to this journey and the exploration of the following pages—at your own pace. With the car loaded, jump into the driver's seat, and begin your trip to your dream home—your Personal Heart Power!

CHAPTER 2

Energies of the Personal Heart

Finding yourself in the home of your heart, your Personal Heart, lit by the energies of fear and love, it's now time to develop a conscious, energetic connection to it. We hope this excites you, although you may feel fear, confusion, resistance, or even no feelings at all. What matters in this moment is you have the awareness of how you are feeling. How you feel now is right for *you*. It's important to start this adventure without judging yourself. Instead, begin with a sense of curiosity about discovering your Personal Heart.

The **Personal Heart is the sensory center for the collective energetic experiences of your thoughts, feelings, and behaviors in relation to the Mode of Fear and Mode of Love.** We refer to these two modes as the **primary vibrational energies.** Which one you operate from in any moment determines your perception of your life.

Our Personal Heart senses energetic information as we experience life. During this journey, we will learn to recognize our life experiences through our thoughts, feelings, and behaviors, as well as what energies are influencing them. So, let's begin with the fundamental energies of fear and love.

We refer to the energies of fear and love as lower and higher vibrations. A lower vibration results when we operate from fear, and a higher vibration occurs when we operate from love. Our Personal Heart is fueled by these lower and higher vibrations. All energies—including sadness, anger, anxiety, guilt, disappointment, gratitude, happiness, security, and hope—can exist in our Personal Heart at any time. If you are interested in learning more about a specific energy scale for feelings, look at the Map of Consciousness created by Dr. David Hawkins in *Power vs. Force*.[6]

Dictionary.com defines energy as "The strength and vitality required to sustain physical or mental activity." Notice: there is no mention of feelings here. We are in an era of expanding the definition of energy to include the experience of feeling. In this book, **energy is the *vibrational frequency we operate from within our Personal Heart: Fear or Love. Vibrational frequency is the range of energies we experience within our Personal Heart.**

This is the time to connect to our feelings in a healthy way. Being aware of our feelings provides us with the information we need to make conscious decisions. Once we are consciously aware of how we are feeling in a particular moment, we can connect to a greater depth of understanding of our true needs. This understanding allows us to make choices that restore or maintain our balance for optimal Personal Heart functioning. Conscious awareness directly influences our decision-making process.

Being more aware of our feelings in our Personal Heart, and of the emotional thoughts in our mind, allows us to operate more consciously in life. It enables us to make optimal choices. Operating in this conscious way with our Personal Heart and mind, in a loving relationship, is what we refer to as operating from our Personal Heart Power. Having more awareness in our heart and mind provides new opportunities for us to process through our thoughts and feelings to create our love-focused life.

Our *Mode of Operation influences our perception of the energies coming into our heart. Our **Mode of Operation refers to how we are managing the range of vibrational energy in our Personal Heart at any given time. This determines whether we are operating from the Mode of Fear or the Mode of Love.** Although the Mode of Operation is a continuum of vibrational frequency, the two primary Modes of Operation in our Personal Heart are the Mode of Fear and the Mode of Love.

We are living in a **Mode of Fear when our Personal Heart is operating primarily with lower vibrational energies.** Conversely, we are living in a **Mode of Love when the Personal Heart is operating primarily with higher vibrational energies.**

Having a conscious relationship with the Modes of Operation can set us free to be our authentic self. When we operate from the Mode of Fear, we contribute the energy of fear to our life. Likewise, we contribute the energy of love to our life when we operate from the Mode of Love. It takes awareness and courage to shift from operating from the Mode of Fear to the Mode of Love.

Our Personal Heart Power is most effective when the Personal Heart and a calm mind are functioning together from the Mode of Love. This means both our heart and our mind are operating from Unconditional Love more often. Unconditional Love is a power that supports, encourages, motivates, and has compassion for ourselves and others.

When the Personal Heart and mind are functioning from the Mode of Fear, they are operating ineffectively. They are operating with fear as a reactionary force that wants to control, dominate, and oppress us and others from living a love-focused life rather than being an informant that wants to support a love-focused life. In this mode, it is more challenging to look inward because fear seeks safety externally. It is a fear-based belief that we need to control, dominate, or oppress, otherwise, someone else will do these things to us. If we live with this fear-driven belief system, then there's a reason why we have established it.

The great news is that we do not need to remain in a fear-based belief system when we desire something different, like true safety and Unconditional Love. Once we recognize that we want our life to be different, we are ready to make the choices that lead to transitions and ultimately *transformation into our Personal Heart Power.

The Mode of Fear and the Mode of Love can be activated from the heart or mind, which determines our Mode of Operation. The HeartMath Institute, a leader in scientific heart research, says, "The heart actually sends more signals to the brain than the brain sends to the heart! Moreover, these heart signals have a significant effect on brain function—influencing emotional processing as well as higher cognitive faculties such as attention, perception, memory, and problem-solving. In other words, not only does the heart respond to the brain, but the brain continuously responds to the heart."[7] For more heart-based research, visit HeartMath.com.

In the mind and Personal Heart relationship, the heart can receive sensory input. It is the sensing and intuitive center. The mind is informed, often subconsciously, through the filters of the Personal Heart. When we're functioning from a fear-focused heart, our mind is informed by the Mode of Fear. Whereas if we function from a love-focused heart, we inform our mind from the Mode of Love. What's important to understand is that each Mode of Operation leads us to interpret the sensory information differently. This is why the same situations can be interpreted and responded to so differently by each person and explains why, in hindsight, we later regret some of the decisions we make. The Mode of Operation greatly affects our perception of life!

We've all been in situations where our words or actions have been completely misunderstood for what we have said or done, or we have misunderstood someone else. This effect causes many conflicts between people, as well as between cultures and nations. It is beneficial to be aware of the Mode of Operation of each person involved, especially in misunderstandings.

Let's imagine you're at an event hosted by a co-worker. Although you are not best friends, you have developed a nice friendship over the years. Occasionally, you socialize outside of work. At the event, your coworker comes up to say, "Hello," right after you've tasted one of her hors d'oeuvres. You enjoyed it so much that you reply with, "I just had the most unusual hors d'oeuvres I have ever tasted!"

She's taken aback. "What do you mean by that?"

"I mean my mouth exploded from all the flavors!" you reply, excitedly.

She frowns. "How can it explode? There aren't even any hot spices in it."

Confused, you try to clarify the situation. "I never said there were hot spices in it."

She lets out a big sigh and walks away.

Confused and irritated, you start a conversation with someone else.

On Monday at work, she passes by your desk and says, "So, you didn't like my hors d'oeuvres, huh?"

Can you see the different ways this scenario could continue to play out, depending on each person's Mode of Operation?

The mind receives sensory information from the Personal Heart for processing and interpreting. It is the thinking and emotional processing center. The Personal Heart receives the lower and higher vibrational energies that come into our heart, and this creates our sensation of feelings. These feelings subsequently inform our mind. This information is based upon our experiences and the Mode of Operation from which our heart is currently operating.

Consciously or unconsciously, our Personal Heart and mind express behaviors from the input of our thoughts and feelings. When we operate from our Personal Heart Power, the expression of behaviors from the Personal Heart and mind are in sync. When they are out of sync, their independent operation can cause inner conflict. This is why gaining awareness from an open Personal Heart perspective is so valuable. The sooner our awareness operates from the Mode of Love, the more likely we will function optimally, in sync with our open Personal Heart and calm mind.

Finding a place to live is a common example of when the heart and mind may be out of sync. There are so many thoughts, feelings, and behaviors that go into this experience. It does not matter if the experience is one of excitement or dread; many of us *toss and turn* in the decision-making process. This often stems from an inner conflict between our Personal Heart and mind.

Perhaps the place you are most excited about is twenty percent more than you had originally planned to spend, and you had already stretched your finances for that budget. The other potentially viable place, and one you can comfortably afford, is an extra thirty-minute drive to and from work—on a good day. Drive time matters in your tightly scheduled life. In addition, the housing market is tight. How your Personal Heart and mind operate together greatly influences the decision you make.

When the heart and mind are working in sync together, they will come to the most optimal decision for us. This is when life feels manageable—even in challenging situations, like finding a home. When the Personal Heart and mind are not in sync, either a struggle ensues or one of them will completely shut down. Either way, it typically makes a big decision-making process less than optimal. This is when life feels overwhelming or unmanageable.

The good news is that when we gain an awareness of how these challenges affect our thoughts, feelings, and behaviors, we are more able to operate from our Personal Heart Power. This shifts these situations into a place of empowerment instead of struggle.

When we were born, we began developing an awareness of love and fear. This awareness evolved depending upon the environment in which we lived and what energies we were exposed to. These energies work in relationship to the physical body's autonomic nervous system.

A brief reminder from our biology class: the autonomic nervous system manages the balance of our nervous system. It includes the sympathetic and parasympathetic nervous systems. The sympathetic nervous system is triggered by fear, and the parasympathetic nervous system is activated by love.

Fear energy, in relationship to the sympathetic nervous system, triggers the fight, flight, or freeze mode of the autonomic nervous system. It's activated when we are in a fearful or stressful situation for a short period of time. However, we can also function in a prolonged triggering of this system when we are living in survival mode with persistent stressors. These can contribute to the sensations or feelings of anger, insecurity, anxiety, avoidance, overwhelm, or other lower vibrational feelings fueled by fear. Over longer periods, the stressors can become chronic, as can the lower vibrational feelings that are triggered.

The sympathetic nervous system is the stress center of our autonomic nervous system. It's designed to protect us from potential dangers in our environment. For many of us, the system continues to be activated long after the danger has gone. This hyper-vigilant mindset creates unnecessary stress, which only perpetuates the perception of danger. For example, if you experience your home burning down, it is reasonable for the sympathetic nervous system to engage in that moment and disengage once the danger is gone. If you cannot process through the fearful feelings of that experience, the fear of another home fire can linger for a long time, which may keep the sympathetic nervous system engaged.

Within the nervous system, Unconditional Love has a relationship with the parasympathetic nervous system. This system restores the autonomic nervous system to balance, to a calm and restored state, by preventing the overworking of the sympathetic nervous system. It does this by slowing it down. It wants us to relax and restore balance to our mind, Personal Heart, and physical body. Therefore, increasing the function of the parasympathetic nervous system is desirable because it returns our nervous system to balance.

To shift from a Mode of Fear to a Mode of Love in our autonomic nervous system, we need to place ourselves in circumstances that decrease the opportunity for triggering lower vibrational thoughts, feelings, and behaviors. We also need to develop skills to manage these lower vibrational thoughts, feelings, and behaviors more effectively. This will decrease our sympathetic nervous system activation. By doing this, our parasympathetic nervous system will be engaged, and the situation will feel more manageable. This enhances our physical balance and calm mental activity, moving us to the Mode of Love. This creates sensations or feelings of joy, love, and happiness in the feel-good center of the autonomic nervous system. Thinking back to our home fire example, once the actual fire experience has passed and we can feel safe again in a new home, our parasympathetic nervous system becomes engaged and we feel a decreased perception of stress.

At the beginning of life, we are born into a household situation that operates primarily from the Mode of Fear or Mode of Love—most likely both. The Mode of Operation in our family primarily depends upon our parents' or caregivers' Mode of Operation. Their Mode of Operation is based upon their perception of life.

For some, childhood is a very loving situation and for others, it can be challenging or even extremely difficult. Most people grow up ebbing and flowing between the Mode of Fear and the Mode of Love. This is the human experience. A Personal Heart that is primarily functioning in the Mode of Fear will experience the world as unsafe and lacking what they need. Similarly, a Personal Heart primarily functioning in the Mode of Love will experience the world as safe and having enough of what they need.

For more insight into your upbringing's relationship with the Mode of Fear and the Mode of Love, take some time to explore the following questions:

- What Mode of Operation seemed to be most prevalent in your family while you were growing up?
- Did each of your caregivers have the same or different Mode of Operation?
- What Mode did you primarily operate from while growing up?
- What Mode do you primarily operate from now?

Take some time to reflect on your answers. Are there any insights that might explain which Mode of Operation you primarily operate from, and why? Don't worry if these are challenging questions to answer now. Once we gain more awareness and understanding of the Modes of Operation, we will have more power to choose the way we would like to operate.

As we grow into adulthood, we learn to interpret the fear and love energies in our Personal Heart. These interpretations can be both a conscious and subconscious process. Our interpretation of fear and love informs our Mode of Operation. This creates our perception of life. Our Mode of Operation continually filters the thoughts and feelings of everything we experience in our life. And this processing completely depends on the choices we do and don't make. There is not another person who will unfold through life the same way as each of us will. How we experience fear and love is unique to us.

Just as you are uniquely you, it helps to recognize that each person operates differently through their Modes of Operations—their unique selves. When we gain a greater awareness of our Mode of Operation, as well as the Mode of Operation of others, we benefit because we can look at ourselves and others differently with compassion and understanding instead of judgment. The Mode we are viewing from creates the reality we see in the world.

For example, if we choose to operate from the Mode of Love, we will learn to look at how we can further enhance the energy of Unconditional Love in our daily life. We will also recognize how we energize fear and how to shift that energy to love. In every choice, fear and love show up. Mostly fear and love show up in the subconscious, and so it fuels automatic behaviors. Locking doors, turning off the stove, putting the milk in the refrigerator, or washing hands—love and fear are there.

Depending upon our Mode of Operation, we either lock the door out of habit or we lock the door because we are afraid someone will come in. We turn off the stove because we finished with it, or we turn off the stove because we worry about a fire. We put the milk in the refrigerator because it keeps it cool and fresh, or we put the milk in the refrigerator because it will go bad if we don't. We wash our hands to keep them clean, or we wash our hands because we are afraid of contaminating something.

These decisions are often subconscious because they have become habits based on our Mode of Operation. If we pause to think about why we make these everyday decisions, we can then consider whether we operate more from the Mode of Fear or the Mode of Love.

Remember, there is no judgment here. Paying more attention to these everyday decisions becomes an opportunity to gain more awareness. This can help us decide if there are changes we would like to make in our Mode of Operation. We can make these decisions totally from fear or totally from love, or on a continuum between the two. Awareness informs our perception regarding our everyday decision-making process.

Imagine moments when you feel worried about the future. You want to control the outcome. You are stuck in overthinking. You believe you are not good enough and you do not feel totally safe in the situation. When I (Grace) felt the desire to start a new business many years ago, I immediately feared my business would fail because I wasn't good enough to run a business. I also worried I would not make enough money to support my family. This fear and worry kept me stuck in overthinking and over-planning.

Most of us can easily imagine feeling this fear about the future. What is challenging for most of us is we do not recognize how it disconnects us from our Personal Heart. Can you see how being stuck in overthinking about the future could make it difficult to connect with your Personal Heart? Our body senses this fear as well. It reacts by tensing up: our jaw tightens, our breathing becomes quick and shallow, our heart rate increases, and we may even experience body pain.

When fear shows up in the Mode of Fear, it can trigger an automatic reaction to the sympathetic nervous system for the fight, flight, or freeze reaction. This limits any opportunity to identify the optimal choices in the moment. This is not the warm and fuzzy feeling we desire to wrap ourselves in. Unconscious patterns of thoughts, feelings, and behaviors, especially rooted in the Mode of Fear, make it difficult to shift towards more loving thoughts, feelings, and behaviors. In this existence, our life is being led by our unconscious living, not our conscious awareness.

However, with the awareness of this feeling of fear, there is still power—the power to change. It is not possible, or beneficial, to get rid of fear altogether. In fact, it can be a welcomed friend. Ideally, we want to build a healthy relationship with fear. A relationship where we live our life from a Mode of Love, but with fear as an informant. When fear informs us, it allows us to determine stressful moments from the Mode of Love. It provides us with information that enables us to make the best choices for ourselves or others at that moment.

Going back to my story, I created a successful business because of the amazing emotional support from my husband, children, family, friends, and clients. Their belief in me, combined with my desire to create a unique center to facilitate healing in others, counterbalanced the fears of failure. When fear showed up, I could reassure myself that things would work out. I knew that this was my work to do, and I made conscious choices to make it happen.

Having the awareness of fear as an informant lets us make conscious choices to shift to the Mode of Love for our life. The desire to feel whole is the desire to connect fully to Unconditional Love within ourselves in our Personal Heart. With this Unconditional Love, we typically feel comfortable, safe, confident, grateful, supported, or energized and self-accepting. This is not perfection; this is acceptance and the desire to love more.

Once we have this awareness, we can choose consciously to shift our Mode of Operation to Love, which will enhance our ability to love ourselves and others more. If you desire a deeper flow of Unconditional Love, then it's time to connect more deeply to your Personal Heart.

CHAPTER 3

Conscious Awareness

To connect consciously to our Personal Heart, we need to become aware of our energetic heart. Awareness is our power! This awareness comes when we intentionally connect our Personal Heart with our calm mind. It takes mental focus to connect consciously. When we have the awareness of how our heart and mind are operating, we can consciously determine if they are out of alignment or in sync with one another. Determining this is functioning with conscious awareness.

However, because it takes effort and focus to connect with conscious awareness, we frequently go about our lives without making conscious decisions. Therefore, our Personal Heart and mind may remain separated more frequently. Our closed heart cannot communicate as effectively with the mind, and the chaotic mind frequently receives the Personal Heart information inaccurately. When we are in the Mode of Love and our heart and mind are in alignment, we feel safer receiving information about the lower vibrational feelings we sense in our Personal Heart. But, when the stressful mind is trapped in our stories about the past or future, it typically rejects the sensory information coming from our Personal Heart. Therefore, when our mind is stuck in past or future thoughts, it's not in the present moment to allow for the conscious awareness of the connection between the mind and Personal Heart.

Many of us want to connect more deeply with ourselves, which requires a conscious awareness. This awareness, in relationship to our Personal Heart, is being cognizant of how our thoughts, feelings, and behaviors influence our Mode of Operation.

Understanding Thoughts

Let's imagine you have a sweet snack of something before going to bed every evening. This is a habit created in childhood, so you do not even think about it—you just do it. Now, well into adulthood, you go for your annual medical checkup, which you have avoided for several years. The doctor advises that you have diabetes. With that comes the recommendation to eliminate your sugar intake for the benefit of your health. That evening, when you go to get your sweet snack, unfamiliar feelings run through your mind and heart as you realize it is not healthy for your body to have these snacks. How you manage these thoughts of disappointment is determined by your Mode of Operation.

When we have a conscious awareness of these thoughts, we have the option to change. It is very difficult to change what we are not aware of. In this process, it is most beneficial to approach the change with a sense of curiosity and non-judgment. These modifications begin with the awareness of our thoughts. With conscious awareness, the next time we grab that sweet evening snack, we're more likely to think about what it's doing to our health. And with that awareness comes power: the power to do what is best for our health or hold on to tradition.

To change, we must make a conscious effort to make a different choice. If we choose to remain the same, we will decide to ignore the doctor's recommendations, and thus our health. This can occur from a conscious or unconscious way of functioning within the mind.

Exploring conscious awareness about our thoughts is one of the most powerful connections we can use to tap into our Personal Heart

Power. Our thoughts determine our perception of reality. The scientific, spiritual, and medical arenas are discovering this as a fact. They're now recognizing how these arenas overlap each other, which benefits our understanding of the power of our thoughts. There are many books written on the topic: *The Power of Intention* by Wayne Dyer;[8] *The Secret* by Rhonda Byrne;[9] and *The Power of Eight* by Lynne McTaggart,[10] to name a few of our favorites. A film on this topic is, *What the Bleep Do We Know!?* by William Arntz, Betsy Chasse, and Mark Vincente.[11]

Our thoughts determine our perception of our life. Whether or not we are aware of our thoughts, the Mode of Fear or the Mode of Love typically filters them. When they are filtered from the Mode of Love, we have thoughts of a higher vibrational frequency than when we operate from the Mode of Fear.

In the lower vibrational frequencies, we process thoughts through a filter of fear. This is when our thoughts tend to be more fearful, pessimistic, closed-minded, judgmental, insensitive, and destructive. This typically puts our mind in a more stressful thought process, creating a desire to overreact, avoid, or shut down. In the higher vibrational thought process, with a filter of love, our thoughts tend to be more loving, optimistic, open to new ideas with different perspectives, less judgmental, more discerning, compassionate, and kind. With this higher vibrational frequency, we typically process these thoughts with a calm mind and open Personal Heart.

The continuum of lower and higher vibrational energies is active as we process our thoughts throughout the day. Having the awareness of our thoughts allows us to influence our desired outcomes intentionally through the choices we make.

Imagine you are at your new dream home and your mom is coming to visit. You are excited to show her around.

"That drive is longer to get here than where you lived before," she says as soon as she arrives, "but what a beautiful drive. I can see why you love it."

You respond, "It is only ten minutes longer, Mom. Does the first thing you say really need to be a complaint?"

She frowns. "I wasn't complaining. I said how beautiful a drive it was."

"Yeah, but not until you complained about how *long* the drive was."

Her frown deepens. "I said how beautiful the drive was!"

"Why are you snapping at me?"

She steps towards the house. "Why don't we just go inside and look at your new house?"

In this example, can you see how your potential fear of judgment has determined your reaction to your mom's comment about the drive?

However, had you been operating in the Mode of Love, you would more likely have responded to her positive comment about the beautiful drive rather than the comment about how long the drive was. Notice how the Mode of Operation affects how we perceive a situation and how perception can affect the outcome of our lives.

But what if Mom was complaining about the long drive? Upon hearing that complaint, and through being aware of our thoughts, we could decide not to react to her irritation. Instead, we could focus on her comment about the beautiful drive. This shows how, when we are conscious of our thoughts, we can shift our focus and choose to create a joyful welcome for our mom.

This is the power of awareness. Becoming more aware of our thought processes will empower us to connect more deeply to our Personal Heart. It also allows us the opportunity to shift our thought process in the moment when it is not aligned with our desired outcomes. This does not mean we can immediately change the circumstances, but it is possible to shift our thought processing from a Mode of Fear to a Mode of Love. At the very least, it offers an expanded awareness of our thoughts.

Understanding Feelings

With this expanded thought awareness, we're embarking on a courageous journey of self-discovery that can lead us directly to our Personal Heart Power. Not only that, but in addition to this greater thought awareness, we may also become more aware of our feelings.

Feeling awareness occurs primarily in our Personal Heart. Just as with our thoughts, our Mode of Operation greatly influences our awareness of our feelings. Again, feelings can occur consciously or subconsciously. Awareness is the moment when we notice something. Consciousness gives our attention to that something.

This practice of awareness in our Personal Heart will bring our feelings to a more conscious level. Conscious awareness increases our *emotional intelligence. **Emotional intelligence is our awareness of our feelings combined with our effective processing of these feelings with our mind**. Our emotional intelligence is our mind and heart working together, which strengthens our Personal Heart Power.

Just like thoughts, feelings have higher and lower vibrational frequencies to them. Ideally, we would remain in higher vibrations to create an optimal balance within our feelings. To do this, we must first become aware of them in any moment. Our feelings move quickly to the mind. Our Personal Heart senses and filters them all the time—we are often unaware of this. If we had to sense each of our feelings with awareness, we would not have time to do anything else! Therefore, when we are not satisfied with how we are feeling in the moment or how we are experiencing life, having an awareness of our feelings is beneficial.

Feelings operate on a wide energetic spectrum, ranging from shame to joy, and are an important part of living life. It is helpful to understand the range of feelings when trying to maintain balance in the Personal Heart. There is a tendency to label them as *good* or *bad*. However, to increase our Personal Heart Power, it is important to leave the labels behind and think of feelings as useful information. Using them as the feedback from our Personal Heart informs our mind of how we are feeling in the present moment. Our feelings are trying to provide information to our mind, so the mind can work with the Personal Heart in the emotional processing for optimal decision making.

When we notice our feelings, we have a conscious decision to make. We will decide if we wish to feel and process through them or to ignore and suppress them. Feelings act like an internal monitor, informing us of the quality of balance in our heart and mind. When we are open to sensing and processing our feelings, it gives us more information to determine what the Personal Heart and mind need in the moment.

When we recognize our feelings as objective information about our mental and physical well-being, our feelings may be more manageable and not so overwhelming. With practice, it's possible to process through our lower vibrational feelings and experience higher vibrational ones as a result! And because these higher vibrational feelings are more desirable, we establish practices that help us rebalance ourselves when we sense we are teetering out of balance. As we operate with our Personal Heart Power, this ability to process our feelings consciously allows us to appreciate all of them.

There are different ways to process through our feelings, and in Section 3, we share some Personal Heart Power Tools that will help you do this effectively. Over time, you'll discover which processing tools work most effectively for you as you bravely embark on acknowledging your feelings without judgment. When you take on more challenging feelings, take a deep breath and find your courage. It's important to remember that when you can consciously connect with your feelings, you are beginning the process to restore your emotional balance.

To illustrate this, we're going to take you on a journey through an experience that will introduce you to a variety of feelings. Be open to and aware of any feelings that arise for you as you read the following story. Your feelings are valuable information for you to understand yourself more deeply. For more awareness, it may be helpful to write down your feelings. Connecting with them creates a healthy relationship if you want an open Personal Heart and calm mind.

A Journey Through an Experience

Imagine waking up in your beach home. It is a beautiful spring morning, and you cannot resist the temptation to go to the nursery and buy flowers for your front yard gardens. When you arrive there, the plethora of colors, blooms, and varieties is enticing. Before you know it, your tray is full, with a beautiful array of floral treasures, and you make your purchase. You feel joyful, grateful, and proud of what will enliven your spring flower gardens.

When you arrive home, you place the flowers near to where you want them, intending to come back later that day and plant them. But it's unusually hot, so you decide to work indoors. As life sometimes plays out, you get sidetracked and completely forget about your plant purchases.

The next morning, you remember your treasured purchases and go outside to plant them. But your excitement and joy quickly vanish. Suddenly, you discover your beautiful blooms have all wilted from yesterday's unseasonal heat.

How do you feel after reading this story? How would you feel if this happened to you? Notice what your feelings are in this moment. Be aware of them. Remember, there's no right or wrong. You just need to recognize the feelings this story has evoked within you.

Here are three examples of the different ways feelings may emerge and be processed regarding this experience. Each example illustrates valid feelings that may emerge from different perspectives of the same situation.

Scenario 1

You experience feelings of sadness and disappointment, and judge yourself, wondering how you could have been so stupid and irresponsible. This trigger is so powerful that it moves you to anger. You pick up the floral treasures and dump them forcibly in the trash. Angry, you go back inside, open the refrigerator, and eat the remaining two pieces of apple pie. After eating, you do not think of the floral treasures again.

In this reactive state, you are not processing your feelings because once self-judgment sets in, feelings tend to shut down. Your knee-jerk reaction to dispose of the pain allows you to quickly move on from these challenging feelings. Eating the pie further disconnects you from your challenging feelings. Eating is one of many numbing behaviors people use to avoid their feelings and processing through them.

Scenario 2

You feel sad and disappointed, but you are half-hearted about what has occurred. It doesn't really register. You are annoyed but have a shoulder-shrugging *whatever* attitude about it. You have developed a bit of an easy-come easy-go attitude which often grows from disappointments regularly occurring and not processing through the feeling of disappointment.

Your judgmental self-talk is not as intense as in the first scenario. Instead, you might think, *Well, I guess those flowers won't bloom this year.* You would probably pick them up with some irritation, toss them out, and go on with your day, not giving the flowers another thought. If you did, you would need to process through your feelings or suppress them.

Scenario 3

You feel sad and disappointed, so you process through these feelings and offer yourself compassion in this circumstance. You honor and recognize the time, money, and effort that was lost from your decision. You then reassure yourself that you can buy more flowers, this time protecting them better.

You offer yourself forgiveness and understanding that you do not control the weather and that sometimes these things occur in life. You realize there is no benefit in judging yourself for the outcome in this situation. Instead, you try salvaging the floral treasures that you can. You care for those that are salvaged and dispose of those that didn't make it. You feel a subtle contentment because you are grateful that some may survive. You buy more plants to fill in for those that were lost.

On any day, you may recognize yourself living any one of these three scenarios, or some variation of them. Our reactions to life events depend upon the situation, the state of our Personal Heart, the state of our mind, and our Mode of Operation in Fear or Love. In these three scenarios, three different *Personal Heart States present themselves. We'll explore the Personal Heart States as a framework for understanding how our Personal Heart is operating in the next chapter.

In each of these scenarios, there are various levels of awareness. Awareness occurs when we choose how to respond or react, either consciously or subconsciously. Our reaction is determined by our Mode of Operation and previous life experiences. Our reaction will determine which scenario we play out.

There are a variety of ways in which we might, or might not, process feelings or react to life's external situations. Becoming aware of this allows us to make choices more aligned with our core beliefs and values. Processing through our feelings with a higher level of conscious awareness allows for the most optimal restoration of emotional balance. Balanced feelings can inform us what behaviors are most beneficial for us in the moment. Having more conscious awareness of our feelings enables us to choose healthier behaviors.

Understanding Behaviors

Just like our thoughts and feelings, behaviors have higher and lower vibrations. It's the vibration of the intention or motivation that determines the behavior we choose. With lower vibrational energy, we are more likely to behave like the scenario where the floral treasures were angrily discarded in the trash.

However, when we experience a moment of awareness in such a situation, we have an opportunity to behave differently. When we feel and process through the lower vibrational feelings, we are more likely to choose a higher vibrational behavior to resolve the stressful situation. In lower vibrational energy, we choose behaviors that numb, ignore, or dramatize the situation, such as in the scenario where the floral treasures were picked up and turned into floral trash. The numbing behavior of eating two pieces of apple pie illustrates actions to suppress the unwanted feelings. Remember, suppressed feelings do not go away. They are likely to arise again.

Whereas, in higher vibrational energy, we feel more content. We are more likely to respond by salvaging our floral treasures. In this higher vibrational energy, our behaviors stay in or return to balance. The ideal response is to maintain a calm mind and open Personal Heart to make choices in our behavior that work for the best outcome. This is a healthy feedback loop that informs us of our thoughts and feelings so we might choose higher vibrational behavior.

Learning how to sense and process our thoughts and feelings with awareness to choose higher vibrational behaviors is new for many of us. Recognize that it is not always easy to process intentionally through our thoughts and feelings. However, when we follow through with the processing, it often brings us to a greater place of understanding and peace within ourselves. This creates a greater strength within us for choosing beneficial behaviors. Awareness also allows us to understand why we behave the way we do.

If we ignore the painful thoughts and feelings, we will push them into a subconscious place and continue with lower vibrational behaviors, aka *bad habits*. These challenging thoughts and feelings either remain in our subconscious until we feel strong enough to process through them consciously, or they get re-triggered with a future stressful event.

We have four primary choices of behavior when thoughts and feelings are re-triggered:

- To process through the challenging ones because we feel safe enough.
- To overreact to the overwhelming ones.
- To push them back down because we don't want to deal with the overwhelming ones.
- To continue ignoring them.

When we can no longer hold these thoughts and feelings down, they will erupt and fuel lower vibrational behaviors. Being aware of this gives us another opportunity to notice them and then process through them consciously or push them into our subconscious again.

Pain, joy, and all other feelings are part of our life. We cannot always change our situations, but we can choose *how* to experience those feelings in those situations. Beginning our transition to a higher consciousness occurs as we become aware of our thoughts, feelings, and behaviors, and we understand our relationship with each of them. In the journey to our Personal Heart Power, becoming more aware of how we feel and how others might feel in the moment is powerful and matters.

When we intentionally choose to live consciously from our Personal Heart, we can recognize if our choices are coming from the Mode of Fear or the Mode of Love. Our Personal Heart will have a different relationship with each mode. In the Mode of Fear, we believe in limited choices. When we function at a totally subconscious level, choices aren't even considered. However, as we learn how to be more consciously aware, we realize that we do have choices.

So, in the Mode of Love, awareness of our thoughts and feelings allows us to see more choices for higher vibrational behavior. It is up to us to choose whether to become more aware. Each choice we make, even the simplest one, originates either consciously or subconsciously from the Mode of Fear or the Mode of Love. What we choose is usually determined by our perception of life. Our perception determines whether things happen *to* us or *for* us. Whatever our current processing procedure is, wherever we are in this process, it is appropriate for us right now.

The good news is that wanting to gain a greater awareness of our thoughts, feelings, and behaviors means we are more likely to develop a greater ability to operate with conscious awareness. This increases our capacity to decide with our Personal Heart Power. It takes desire, commitment, and determination, but remember—you are brave. You are developing your awareness of your Personal Heart.

In the next chapter, we will look at the various Personal Heart States, which will help us understand how conscious awareness affects which state we are in.

CHAPTER 4

The Five Personal Heart States

We have explored how the Modes of Operation influence the Personal Heart. It's by becoming consciously aware of whether we're operating from the Mode of Fear or the Mode of Love that allows us to make more beneficial choices in our thoughts, feelings, and behaviors. These beneficial choices create our Personal Heart Power.

Our Mode of Operation is not a binary state: that of Fear or Love. Instead, we like to think of it as a continuum, with Fear at one end and Love at the other. As we become more aware of our Mode of Operation, there may be times when we're unsure of where we are along the continuum. To help determine this, we have identified five Personal Heart States:

- Disconnected,
- Reactive,
- Half-hearted,
- Content,
- and Whole.

Each Personal Heart State reflects how our Personal Heart is operating in connection to the energies of fear and love. It is the qualities and quantities of the energies' vibrational frequencies within the Personal Heart that determine our Personal Heart State.

These Personal Heart States depend upon our Mode of Operation, the vibrational frequency, the quality, and quantity of energy in the Personal Heart, as well as the situation. Typically, we have a primary Heart State that we operate from. However, we can also operate in each of these Personal Heart States at different times. Our operating state can fluctuate frequently or remain relatively consistent.

Exploring our Personal Heart through these five different states helps us to understand our current perception of life. Our Mode of Operation sets the energetic frequency—Fear or Love—for our perception of life. Our Personal Heart Power is our ability to:

- sense our current feelings,
- use our conscious awareness to recognize our thoughts,
- process through those feelings and thoughts,
- make choices for higher vibrational behaviors,
- and recognize the Personal Heart State we are currently in.

Using our Personal Heart Power in this way allows us to operate from the most effective Personal Heart State for that moment.

Remember, it is our relationship and perspective to our experiences, not the experiences themselves, that determine our Personal Heart State. This explains why different people have different experiences in the same situation. It is common to shift in and out of various states depending upon the situation and our perspective of it. We have perceptions that determine our opinions in life.

Opinions are fueled by fear or love. When fueled by fear, judgment has taken over. When fueled by love, it is discerning. Judgment of ourselves and others sabotages our ability to live a love-focused life, while discernment supports a love-focused life.

Being aware of which Personal Heart State we're currently in gives us choices. Once we know which state we're operating from, we can then decide if this is the state we would like to stay in. Having this awareness allows us to make conscious choices to support our decision. It also helps us to use our knowledge effectively to shift our state to one that maintains the optimal balance between the calm mind and Personal Heart.

It is tempting to judge ourselves or others in the lower vibrational heart states. However, this is not beneficial. It would be beneficial to use the information to begin practices that shift us toward higher vibrational heart states.

The Disconnected Personal Heart State

The **Disconnected Personal Heart State feels completely disconnected from the Mode of Love and entirely connected to the Mode of Fear. The Personal Heart is operating from the lowest vibrational thoughts, feelings, and behaviors.** Like all the Personal Heart States, there is a range or spectrum of varying degrees of disconnection. Typically, in the Disconnected Heart State, the range of experiences is numbness through to extreme overwhelm.

Most readers who find themselves in this state will be at the extremely overwhelmed end of the Disconnected continuum. At this end of the continuum, medical support may not be necessary to reconnect to a more loving Personal Heart, but it may still be useful. *If you have a harmful thought toward yourself or others, seek medical support immediately.* When we recognize we are in this Disconnected Personal Heart State, it is important to do so without judgment. Having no judgment allows us to learn how we might reconnect in our Personal Heart from the Mode of Love. This is a very challenging Personal Heart State, so it is most beneficial to be patient with ourselves and seek help from supportive sources.

In this state, our lower vibrational thoughts tend to spin into one or more *Stress Loops, getting us stuck in past or future scenarios. A **Stress Loop is when the mind is ruminating in thoughts about the past or future, which are anchored by a certain *stressful belief. A stressful belief is one that supports a lower vibrational belief system.** It's by becoming aware of our stressful beliefs that we can change them towards higher vibrational beliefs.

A Stress Loop often results from emotional, physical, and other traumatic experiences throughout life, or even just one stressful event in childhood. A childhood stressful event typically produces overwhelming lower vibrational feelings that a young Personal Heart and mind cannot process through effectively at that time.

Our mind creates Stress Loops to avoid feeling the undesired lower vibrational feelings in our Personal Heart and mind. It is challenging to think and feel in the same moment. We will often choose thinking over feeling because we do not want to feel the lower vibrational feelings. Typically, Stress Loops operate on a subconscious level. Periodically, they're consciously triggered by similar stressful events. We can shift from stressful beliefs to reassuring beliefs when we develop the awareness of lower vibrational feelings and can process through them effectively.

Remember in my (Grace) story when my dad told me I would not be Miss America? As a four-year-old, I believed I couldn't win because something was wrong with me. I did not have the knowledge that the probability of anyone winning was extremely low. This was a stressful event where I was not emotionally capable of processing my feelings. The Stress Loop *I'm not good enough* was created. This Stress Loop encoded the stressful belief, *I am not good enough because of my crooked face.* It was activated whenever physical beauty mattered until the conversation I had with my grandmother in my thirties. That conversation began the healing practice of replacing the stressful belief with reassuring beliefs. I had the awareness, ability, support, and courage to process through the feelings created by the stressful belief.

Can you recognize how the Stress Loop can be triggered again, later on in our lives, when another stressful event triggers the same lower vibrational feelings that our mind or heart doesn't want to feel and process through in that moment? Lower vibrational thoughts ramp up our chaotic mind and close our Personal Heart. The present moment is extinguished by these chaotic stories of the past or future ruminating in our mind. We know that, in the Mode of Fear, lower vibrational feelings are typically dealt with by fight, flight, or freeze to avoid feeling them. Therefore, when we find ourselves in this state, we might refuse to take part in the present moment because the painful feelings are so intense that they feel intolerable. In this state, we are less likely to process these feelings.

The inability to process feelings triggers more fear energy, which further fuels the activation of the sympathetic nervous system (fight, flight, or freeze). In this Disconnected State, the fear energy triggers the Personal Heart and mind to disconnect to a certain degree from one another and unconsciously shuts out other potential choices in that moment. This usually leads to actions that attempt to numb or avoid the lower vibrational feelings.

We might do this by:
- overeating sugar, fat, carbs, etc.,
- excessive drinking,
- smoking,
- drugs,
- inappropriate use of medications,
- overthinking,
- overspending,
- too much technology,
- over-exercising,

- overworking,
- too much sleeping,
- and any other ways to numb.

In this Personal Heart State, we just don't want to feel anything. Instead, we think of ways to avoid the pain and stress, rather than processing through the lower vibrational feelings and dealing with the stressors to get back to balance.

In fact, in this state, we often feel that there are no rational choices. We convince ourselves that the stressful beliefs of our Stress Loops are true. Such beliefs include:

- *I am not good enough.*
- *I am not worthy.*
- *I am not lovable.*
- *I should be perfect.*
- *I should rescue others.*
- *I am powerless.*
- *My needs don't matter, etc.*

It's easy to see how these stressful beliefs can cause worry and anxiety.

Fear fuels lower vibrational behaviors in the Disconnected Personal Heart State and usually causes more imbalance on physical, sensing, energetic, and spiritual levels. We perceive life is against us. This puts us into the judging Stress Loop by judging ourselves, others, and the situation we are in. We are using judging and blaming as behaviors to numb our pain. The stressful mind wants to disconnect from lower vibrational and overreactive feelings in the Personal Heart because it perceives that processing through the feelings is too challenging.

If you find yourself in the Disconnected Personal Heart State most of the time, seek help, support, and guidance. This is not a state to work through alone, especially when your health is affected. Life feels miserable in the Disconnected Personal Heart State.

The Reactive Personal Heart State

The **Reactive Personal Heart State operates mainly from lower vibrational thoughts, feelings, and behaviors, from the Mode of Fear. However, it is not completely disconnected from the Mode of Love. The range of experiences in this Personal Heart State is from overwhelming to stressful.**

At times like this, we may have an occasional awareness of the present moment, but we are still primarily in the past or future thoughts and probably in a Stress Loop. This is more likely to happen when we have not yet learned how to process through our lower vibrational feelings effectively. When stressful situations occur, the reactive mind responds with lower vibrational thoughts, triggering our Stress Loops, and their stressful beliefs. As the lower vibrational thoughts ramp up, this causes more chaos in our mind and closes our Personal Heart in this state. Typically, this triggers an over-reaction rather than a disconnection to feelings.

Our thoughts in this Personal Heart State react to the situation. Our mind and Personal Heart are minimally connected in this state. We cannot think clearly and reasonably in this present moment because we are not anchored in our calm mind and open Personal Heart. Our beliefs about ourselves, others, or the situation are stressful, easily triggering further Stress Loops. This is also not a comfortable state to be in. We are mainly operating in the fight, flight, or freeze mode, although not as intensely as the Disconnected Personal Heart State. We may have a spark of hope that things could be different, even if we feel we're unable to make that happen.

In the Reactive Personal Heart State, our feelings are lower vibrational, out of balance, and overreactive in nature. This happens when our mind cannot process through the lower vibrational feelings effectively in the moment.

Examples of out-of-balance and overreactive feelings are when anger turns into hostility, sadness shifts into depression, fear becomes anxiety, guilt changes to shame, and disappointment turns into hopelessness.

In hindsight, we may regret and wonder how we could have handled the stressful situation differently. However, our overreactive feelings prevent us from maintaining a sense of emotional balance and a calm mind.

Think about the story of the floral treasures earlier. In the first scenario, we felt immediate sadness and disappointment, followed by anger. The anger resulted in us dumping the flowers and eating two pieces of pie to numb the painful feelings. This scenario illustrates how the reactive heart may respond to a stressful event with overreactive feelings and lower vibrational behaviors.

Even though the situational stress in this Reactive State is less stressful than when in the Disconnected Personal Heart State, it still causes a sense of being overwhelmed and out of balance. Our lower vibrational behavior is reactive, which often further increases the stress in the situation. In this state, we take things personally, even when it is not about us.

Think back to the comment about the long drive made by the mom in our story and the different choices we had to react to that. Our reactive behaviors will guide us to make choices based on short-term gains for comfort rather than long-term balance. Similarly, when someone gobbles up five chocolate chip cookies after a partner's judgmental and hurtful comments, they're doing it for the immediate comforting feeling this offers. Instead, it would be better to take the time to process through those painful feelings that may help restore our emotional balance and set healthy limits with our partner's comments. Be kind to yourself when this is not possible.

If we are in this state, it's usually because there are stressful beliefs that have been activated by a challenging situation, or we have attachments to certain outcomes, making it nearly impossible to go with the flow in life. We often blame ourselves or others for our situation in life, concluding that there is nothing we can do to change it for the better. In fact, we frequently believe we have very limited choices and are being told what to do. In this situation, we're completely unaware of the effect our overreaction has on this limited Personal Heart and mind connection.

Sometimes, we notice the outcome of our lower vibrational behavior after we have acted on the situation. It is the *Oops, I should not have done that* awareness. Our Mode of Operation is primarily Fear. If any love is present, it is usually conditional love for ourselves, others, and the world. **Conditional love is love with prerequisites or expectations.** It is when there is a belief that love needs to be earned by doing something *good*, not doing something *bad*, or by doing whatever is expected of yourself and others. Perception of conditional love is limited by the stressful beliefs in our Stress Loops. Overall, life feels reactionary and stressful in this Reactive Personal Heart State.

The Half-Hearted Personal Heart State

Our framework for the Half-hearted Heart State differentiates half-hearted in the Mode of Fear and half-hearted in the Mode of Love. When we're being half-hearted in fear, we are lacking enthusiasm and interest. In love, we are more enthusiastic and interested. So, the **Half-hearted Personal Heart State is when we shift freely between operating from the Mode of Fear and the Mode of Love in our Personal Heart, depending on our perception of the current situation. We ebb and flow between lower and higher vibrational thoughts, feelings, and behaviors. Our range of experience is on a continuum, ranging from less stressful**

to somewhat manageable, often swinging like a pendulum depending on our perception of the situation.

In the Half-hearted Personal Heart State, sometimes we see our life as half-full and we feel grateful for our life. While at other times, we see our lives as half-empty and we feel like life is not going our way, or we do not have enough of something. This lack of something could be money, time, love, energy, or resources. We would like our life to be different because it does not always provide contentment. These thoughts can trigger a Stress Loop. When we're consciously aware of this trigger, we can then take steps to stop ourselves from slipping into the Reactive Personal Heart State.

There is a stronger connection between the heart and mind in this state. This enables the exchange of sensing information between the heart and mind for more effective emotional processing. This connection is a two-way process, which means once the Personal Heart has passed on this information to the mind, the mind can process it and feedback information to the Personal Heart. This is where Personal Heart Power begins.

Our thoughts, feelings, and behaviors also influence our perceptions in this Half-hearted Personal Heart State. When fueled by the Mode of Fear, our thoughts can lead to overthinking, distracting us from the present moment. Depending on our Mode of Operation, we may oscillate between lower and higher vibrational thoughts.

In this Half-hearted State, our thoughts can distract us and pull us in multiple directions as fear and love vie for the primary Mode of Operation. We have a sense of juggling our thoughts, hoping we do not drop the ball on anything. Fear can sneak in and make us believe there is not enough time, money, energy, or resources to accomplish all our responsibilities.

The Mode of Love prevails in our thoughts when there is a sense of less juggling, and those thoughts are primarily higher vibrational in nature. This allows for a calmer mind. In the present moment, we can feel more connection between our Personal Heart and mind in the Mode of Love in this Half-hearted State.

Our feelings in this state fluctuate between being in balance and being slightly out of balance, but not overreactive. The variety of feelings is manageable in this state. We might feel a little angry, sad, or fearful, but not hostile, depressed, or anxious. We may feel grateful, happy, safe, or hopeful, but not feel joy or bliss.

This is an opportune Personal Heart State to process through our lower vibrational feelings to find a more optimal emotional balance. When we're in this state, we usually feel good enough. Stress is tolerable, and life is manageable, but we also yearn for something better. It is uncomfortable to feel the essential pains of life in this state, but we begin to recognize them and understand that we need to process through them. If we keep our feelings somewhat in balance in this state, then we will prevent going into the Reactive Personal Heart State.

As a result, we behave more rationally and logically with a sense of purpose. We're still influenced by the external situations in our life, but we have a partial alignment of the Personal Heart and mind working together, and this optimizes higher vibrational choices. Although we know we have choices, sometimes they are rooted in fear and judgment and sometimes in love and discernment.

Our decision-making process is influenced by whether we are currently behaving from a fearful half-heart or loving half-heart. In the Mode of Love, we have more high-vibrational beliefs that can activate *reassuring beliefs. A **reassuring belief is a higher vibrational belief.**

Choosing higher vibrational behaviors that focus on long-term gains can restore balance more effectively by shifting us into the Mode of Love or keeping us there. In this mode, we make more consistent, higher vibrational choices that help us follow through with a plan to restore or maintain balance.

In the Half-hearted Personal Heart State, we have an opportunity to work on, develop, and discover physical, emotional, energetic, and spiritual balance. We can implement strategies and behaviors to connect our heart to a calmer mind. Our conscious efforts toward balance will determine our ability to shift into the next Personal Heart State: the *Content Personal Heart State.

The Content Personal Heart State

In the **Content Personal Heart State, we operate primarily from the Mode of Love and we use fear as an informant. We primarily function with higher vibrational thoughts, feelings, and behaviors. The range of experiences tends to be on a continuum from manageable to fulfilled, with the ability to remain present in the current moment more often.** In this state, we feel good and satisfied with our life. Mostly, life is easier because we have more abilities to maintain an open Personal Heart and calm mind. These abilities allow us to stay in balance more often.

We enjoy our daily life. This means we've developed a balanced and consistent relationship between the open Personal Heart and calm mind. They work together in nearly full alignment. We can manage life easily, even when it is stressful and challenging. When a Stress Loop presents itself, we typically process through the lower vibrational feelings effectively and find a reassuring belief, so we remain in balance in the Content Personal Heart State.

We can enjoy the earned rewards of being present in the moment more of the time. We lessen our focus on external stressors, knowing that the Personal Heart and mind alignment gives us the power to make higher vibrational choices in this state. We actually desire to resolve stressful situations and get back into balance as needed. Being in balance is a priority in this state and allows for authentic contentment.

We are aware of our higher vibrational thoughts around the experiences we have in life. As a result, we are not easily affected by external circumstances and can maintain balance even in more challenging situations. We have reached the ability to remain present in the moment most of the time. We notice fewer stressful stories in our head that pull us out of the present moment. Life is on our side, and we know it.

Our feelings in a Content Personal Heart State are primarily higher vibrational in nature. Higher vibrational feelings—including gratitude, security, happiness, hope, love, and peace—flow easily in the heart. The lower vibrational feelings of sadness, fear, disappointment, and anger are messengers that something needs our attention.

In the Content Personal Heart State, we accept and can manage and process through lower vibrational feelings effectively to allow them to pass. Our ability to feel and process through more feelings allows us to strengthen the connection between our open Personal Heart and calm mind. This is Personal Heart Power!

In this Content Personal Heart State, we continue developing and maintaining our optimal practices to process through our lower vibrational feelings so we can maintain an emotional and mental balance. Through the conscious awareness of our thoughts, feelings, and behaviors, we can see more clearly how we are creating our perception of life. This state empowers and allows healthier connections with ourselves and others. Life feels content and full of possibilities in this state. It also allows a deeper Personal Heart and mind connection to the Source of Unconditional Love that can shift us into the *Whole Personal Heart State.

The Whole Personal Heart State

In the **Whole Personal Heart State, we are operating from the Mode of Love and feeling connected with the Source of Unconditional Love. We function with higher vibrational thoughts, feelings, and behaviors. There is no range of experience, it is enlightenment: an experience of wholeness**

and oneness, where the illusion of separation from the Source of Unconditional Love and others no longer exists. The key to the Whole Personal Heart State is accepting that separation from Unconditional Love or others is an illusion.

The perception of separation makes it difficult to stabilize the Whole Heart State. This is why this state is so elusive to us. People have been yearning for this connection for eternity. We may experience moments of the Whole Personal Heart State but it is very challenging to live in this state continually.

When we live in the Whole Personal Heart State, we operate consciously from the Mode of Love and connect with the Source of Unconditional Love. We know we are loved unconditionally and we are loving. In this state, there is a complete union with the Source of Unconditional Love. That's how we emerge into the Whole Personal Heart State.

This is where we fully trust the Source of Unconditional Love, accepting that it will provide clarity in what we need in each moment of our life. There is total alignment between the open Personal Heart and calm mind. The oneness of life permeates our consciousness; we think, feel, and act from the wholeness of Unconditional Love.

There is no influence from the external world because we no longer recognize it as separate from ourselves. This knowing of oneness is felt in a higher vibrational connection with the Source of Unconditional Love. When we experience this Personal Heart State, our heart and calm mind are in optimal union.

Our thoughts focus on oneness and merge with the Source of Unconditional Love. In this state, we no longer see other people as separate from us, and we know they are as important as we are. We have shifted from focusing solely on our Personal Heart to engaging with the Global Heart.

All Personal Hearts around the world connect to create the Global Heart. The **Global Heart is the collective energy of the world's**

individual Personal Hearts. When the majority of Personal Hearts operate from the Mode of Love, the Global Heart can shift into *Global Heart Power. **Global Heart Power is when the world's collective Personal Hearts are in community and primarily functioning from their Personal Heart Power from the Mode of Love.** This loving world begins with us as we consciously choose to learn, understand, and develop our Personal Heart Power.

Imagine a world where people have collectively evolved to the highest vibrational energy within their Personal Hearts. Imagine all hearts connecting in a loving way, collectively creating a love-focused world: a world where people have agreed upon a basic framework to understand one another in the Mode of Love. This framework provides a collective understanding of Personal Heart Power and how that power can transform our lives and the lives of others.

In this Whole Personal Heart State, we have fully aligned our Personal Heart and calm mind so that all thoughts and feelings are simultaneously processed to carry out higher vibrational behaviors that are solely rooted in Unconditional Love. We have found our holy grail! We are fully living in Personal Heart Power!

In the Whole Personal Heart State, we feel whole and joyful. We sense all feelings and know they are valuable to our life experiences. Learning how to experience and process them fluidly occurs in this Whole Personal Heart State. We also have a greater understanding of *why* we experience them.

What's important is that we experience our range of vibrational feelings without judgment. We'll experience our feelings fully and with vulnerability because we know they are valuable to our evolution as a human being. Pain is recognized and can be transformed with Unconditional Love so it becomes informative rather than crippling. Our feelings validate our aliveness on our loving journey.

Our behavior is motivated by love and gratitude for what we have received from the Source of Unconditional Love. We extend compassion, kindness, empathy, understanding, acceptance, forgiveness, gratitude, and love freely to all. We are in the world, but not of the world, as we feel led by the Source of Unconditional Love. We make higher vibrational choices through the Mode of Unconditional Love versus choices made through the Mode of Fear. We do not have any expectations or attachments to outcomes; instead, we go with the flow of Unconditional Love. In this state, we experience and function in our life from the complete wholeness of Unconditional Love.

The purpose of life's experiences is neither good nor bad. There is no judgment, only discernment in this heart state. All experiences are happening for us. Maintaining this Whole Personal Heart State requires an uninterrupted connection to and operating with the Source of Unconditional Love. Life feels joyful, whole, and complete in this Personal Heart State.

Further Discussion

Using the framework of the Personal Heart States, we can start making choices that help us shift to a higher vibrational Personal Heart State. These states allow us to operate from our Personal Heart Power. Like with all beneficial things, we must consciously face challenges to learn to manage the connection between our Personal Heart and mind.

Knowing which Personal Heart State we're in gives us valuable information that enables us to shift into a more desirable state. With this awareness, we have a greater possibility to create a love-focused life. We can move into creating the life we desire instead of feeling controlled by life. Over time and with heart-focused practices, we can become more proficient in shifting our Personal Heart States in the moment with ease and grace.

Proficiency requires intention and consistency. Proficiency happens when we use effective tools to move us to a more balanced and loving Personal Heart connected to our calm mind. We cover tools extensively in Section 3.

When we are aware of our Personal Heart State, we can use this knowledge to create the desired outcomes we want in our life. This awareness is especially useful when we find ourselves in the Disconnected or Reactive Heart States. The sooner we recognize these two Personal Heart States, the quicker we can choose to shift out of them and back to a higher vibrational state.

Remember, knowledge is power and gives us the opportunity to change if we choose. There is no judgment in which Personal Heart State we find ourselves. But with this knowledge, we have the choice to determine whether we want to make the required effort to shift to another state.

Through practice and intention, we can gain awareness of others' Personal Heart States. This awareness helps us to set healthy limits as needed, with others, if we do not feel safe in the moment. Knowing our Personal Heart State and the other person's Personal Heart State gives us the power to create reassuring beliefs for ourselves, others, and life. Having a conscious awareness of the five Personal Heart States helps us develop our Personal Heart Power.

Remember, the Personal Heart and mind fluctuate in lower and higher vibrational energies, consciously and subconsciously, as life ebbs and flows. This ebbing and flowing influences the Personal Heart State. We do this every day—knowingly and unknowingly. So, with conscious awareness, we have the power to change our Personal Heart State so we can live our love-focused life.

CHAPTER 5

The Four Personal Heart Chambers

A *Personal Heart Chamber is a particular aspect of the Personal Heart. There are four Personal Heart Chambers: **Energetic, Physical, Sensing, and Spiritual. Each Chamber has a unique function,** but it also functions in relation to the other chambers to keep the Personal Heart in balance. These chambers affect *everything* in our life. Therefore, it is vital that we understand them and create an optimal balance within each of them.

A useful way of visualizing these chambers is to think back to our dream home. Previously, we were standing outside, but now it's time to step inside. Consider each Personal Heart Chamber as a room, and just like any property, its longevity requires regular maintenance. How we decorate those rooms, what we allow in, and what we leave out, is what turns a house into a home. The same is true for our Personal Heart Chambers, for these create and influence the inner environment of our Personal Heart and, depending on how they are expressed, will determine our perception of life.

As we learn how to care for and nurture these four chambers, our beach home will become more balanced and, thus, a place we love to call home.

The Personal Heart Energetic Chamber

The *Personal Heart Energetic Chamber contains the energetic continuum of the vibrational frequencies in the Mode of Fear and the Mode of Love, and how they interact through our thoughts, feelings, and behaviors energetically.

David R. Hawkins, in *Power vs. Force*, created the *Map of Consciousness*, which depicts the various energy field frequencies of the different levels of consciousness.[12] The energy field is the accumulation and summation of the energetic vibrations from our thoughts, feelings, and behaviors. Put simply, the energy field is the amount of fear or love we feel in the moment. Expanding on this energetic field includes all similar energetic feelings of fear and love. Each Mode has its own energetic filters that generate specific vibrational frequencies through our thoughts, feelings, and behaviors. The Energetic Chamber, which houses the Mode of Fear and the Mode of Love, is the energetic gatekeeper of your Personal Heart.

We know that the Mode of Fear resonates at lower vibrational frequencies and the Mode of Love resonates at higher vibrational frequencies. Therefore, to sustain the Mode of Fear, our thoughts, feelings, and behaviors need to resonate in the lower vibrational energies. Even our perception of fear becomes a self-fulfilling prophecy, causing a continuing lower vibrational perception of life in the Mode of Fear. The consequences of having sustained fear in the Energetic Chamber include things like depleted energy, fatigue, chaotic energy, and frenetic energy, even to the point of exhaustion. When the Energetic Chamber is low in energy, it cannot adequately fuel the other chambers. This could lead to an imbalance in the other three Personal Heart Chambers as well. Remember, with awareness and the use of tools, perceptions, and support, we can make choices that can shift the Personal Heart, including the chambers, towards higher vibrational energies.

When the Mode of Love is the gatekeeper of the Energetic Chamber, our thoughts, feelings, and behaviors resonate in the higher vibrational energies. We feel revitalized, energized, alive, well-rested, light-hearted, content, and have an overall sense of balanced energy. This contributes optimally to the other Personal Heart Chambers because this high energy supports the balance in our Personal Heart Energetic Chamber. Once we experience the higher vibrational energies more frequently, the effort to maintain higher vibrations becomes easier and the rewards more desirable.

The Personal Heart Physical Chamber

The ***Personal Heart Physical Chamber relates to the physical status of the entire physical body and is affected by the Mode of Love and the Mode of Fear.** Our Mode of Operation determines the energy in our Physical Chamber. The quality and quantity of this energy supports the physical body, which includes the mind. For example, if you had a good night's sleep, you are more likely to have higher vibrational quality and quantity of energy to support your physical body. The opposite is true if you do not get enough sleep.

In this chamber, the Mode of Fear triggers a more stressful functioning. Overwhelming fear can activate the sympathetic nervous system (the fight, flight, or freeze mode). When we don't manage our fear in a healthy way, our body is physically compromised by its inability to function effectively.

Many of us know of a time in our lives when stress adversely affected our physical health in some way. This may have manifested itself through increased breathing and heart rates, muscle aches and pains, difficulty sleeping, headaches, or aches in other parts of the body. Any discomfort in our physical body can be an indicator the body is not in balance. Ignoring these physical symptoms of imbalance in the early stages may lead to more chronic health situations. At extreme levels of body imbalance, it can feel physically intolerable. This discomfort is an indicator from our physical body and stressful mind that we need to pay attention to and take the necessary steps to restore balance in the Physical Chamber.

This played out in my (Michelle) life on the morning I woke up ten pounds heavier than the night before. In hindsight, I had many messages from my Personal Heart that my life was not in balance before the weight gain, but I was too disconnected from myself to do anything with them. It was the Mode of Fear that was keeping me from doing anything. Once my body spoke so loudly, I recognized fear was informing me to save myself. I spent many months communicating with medical professionals, only to find no reason for my health issues. In the process, I put on forty-five pounds and I ached all over. I was scared. The good news was that I was not dying from anything they could discover through medical testing. But the stressful belief dominating my thoughts was, *I am dying of something.*

I did not want to believe I was dying because I was young and in the prime of my life. I decided I was going to live, if possible. I discovered the reasons for my physical challenges. It was the lower vibrational energies I did not want to deal with in my Personal Heart. I was no longer willing to live like that. I choose compassion and self-care for myself. I needed to put myself first. I am grateful for all the Personal Heart Power wisdom learned from this experience. On one level, I felt like I was going through this alone, and on another level, I knew I had the support of my family and friends. I gained awareness of the support each person can offer in relation to what they are going through in their lives. However, there was nothing more supportive than my connection to the Source of Unconditional Love. The inner guidance through prayer and meditation provided the steps I needed to take to shift to the Mode of Love and balance my Physical Heart Chamber.

None of the physical outcomes of fear sound desirable when we are out of balance, which is an incentive to look at how love can influence the Personal Heart Physical Chamber. When functioning in the Mode of Love, we are more likely to experience more self-care to maintain our optimal health and well-being. We make time for higher vibrational physical activities, including healthy eating, proper sleeping patterns, exercise, seeking medical and other health practitioner support if needed, or whatever we feel would enhance our overall physical health. When it is a stressful mind that's causing our imbalance, seeking supportive mental health practices like meditation and counseling can improve our physical health, too.

When we reach the practice of connecting even deeper into Unconditional Love for ourselves, we begin to operate from a conscious awareness of this Unconditional Love. This motivates us to take care of ourselves even more. When we take good care of ourselves, we experience the physical benefits: optimal heart rates and rhythms, normal blood pressure, minimal or no muscle aches and pains, better sleep cycles, fewer head-and-body aches, a calm mind, and an overall sense of well-being throughout our physical body.

We become more aware of an imbalance in the Physical Chamber as we age. Such imbalances may have been whispering for quite some time, which is why awareness is so beneficial. It allows us to recognize more healthy choices we can make to improve our physical status before it becomes more harmful to our overall well-being.

The Personal Heart Sensing Chamber

The ***Personal Heart Sensing Chamber contains the sensing of feelings within our Personal Heart and sends feeling information to the mind. The Personal Heart Sensing Chamber is supported energetically by the Mode of Fear and the Mode of Love.** When the Sensing Chamber is in balance in the Mode of Love, our feelings connect with our calm mind so that we experience and process them fully. When this happens, our mind interprets them as emotions and can then process those feelings effectively.

When the Sensing Chamber is in the Mode of Fear, this feeling information can become distorted due to past experiences. This distortion leads to misunderstandings or misinterpretations, and so chaos and confusion may arise. When there is a disconnect between the heart and mind, we often attempt to numb and avoid these challenging feelings. Recognizing when this chamber is out of balance is the best time to put into practice the tools to restore the balance. Section 3 provides the tools and practices for the effective processing of feelings to restore balance in this chamber.

To consciously connect to the Sensing Chamber, we must have a spark of awareness. Once aware, we can choose consciously to process through the lower vibrational feelings to rebalance the Personal Heart with higher vibrational feelings. Without conscious awareness, our Personal Heart subconsciously operates in the way it is familiar with, from the Mode of Fear or the Mode of Love.

The Sensing Chamber is in balance when it is open to processing feelings with a calm mind through the Mode of Love. We are more likely to maintain a balance within our feelings by utilizing certain tools and practices, which allow us to process through our lower vibrational feelings and restore balance. When the Mode of Fear dominates this chamber, it creates a heightened sense of fear.

Fear does not allow for healthy processing or expression of our feelings because it is too powerful when it dominates. This is when fear becomes a crippler in our life. It limits our perspective of life. It restricts our Personal Heart to lower vibrational feelings and restrains access to the mind for processing, which puts us in the fight, flight, or freeze response for managing those feelings.

This creates a further imbalance in the Sensing Chamber, leading to lower vibrational feelings, fueling anxiety, phobias, avoiding feelings, or staying stuck in compulsive thoughts. In the extremes of fear, we cannot recognize—much less enjoy—any moment that might typically elicit higher vibrational feelings and thoughts.

When a birthday party is thrown for us, and we are feeling the joy and love of friends and family, we are sensing the celebration with love. If the celebration brings on feelings of dread and worry, then fear is the Mode of Operation and we cannot enjoy the celebration.

Fear blinds us to the beauty of life, which is why it is so important to process through our lower vibrational feelings with a calm mind to restore the balance in the Sensing Chamber.

When there is balance in this chamber, love and other higher vibrational feelings can recalibrate the Personal Heart. Balance allows us to feel Unconditional Love for ourselves and others. We feel gratitude, joy, security, self-confidence, cheerfulness, optimism, and mental well-being with experiences such as the birthday party thrown for us with love and celebration.

When our Mode of Operation is Love, we can also experience higher vibrational feelings through a challenging situation, like the passing of a loved one. Being in the Mode of Love allows us to process through the feelings rather than resisting or getting stuck in them. The sadness, pain, and sense of loss are still there, but our balanced processing comes from a connected open Personal Heart and calm mind. We can recognize that grief is a natural feeling when losing someone we love and we understand that it takes more time to process some of the more intense feelings. Managing feelings as they arise with healthy practices maintains a more balanced Personal Heart Sensing Chamber.

The Personal Heart Spiritual Chamber

The *Personal Heart Spiritual Chamber contains our perception, our ability, and the quality of our connection to the Source of Unconditional Love. This is about connecting to a power of Unconditional Love greater than ourselves. Previously, this connection has been left to religious leaders, gurus, and spiritual teachers to tell us what we need to do to have a connection to the Source of Unconditional Love. Now we realize that each of us can connect to the Source of Unconditional Love directly. This enhances and stabilizes a love-focused life.

The Source of Unconditional Love is connected to us, whether we are consciously aware of our connection or not. Our awareness determines our perception of this loving connection. With an open Personal Heart, we can sense it. It is easier to sense love when we're operating in the Mode of Love. Think of it as the quality of the lighting you perceive in your dream home. You can sense the difference between when the sun is shining brightly through your windows or if there are heavy curtains filtering the sun. This changes your perception of sunlight, but it does not change the intensity of the sunlight.

At this time, you may or may not comprehend this connection to Unconditional Love. It varies greatly from one person to the next. However, no matter where you are on your journey, know that Unconditional Love is there, connected to you. This journey is about gaining more awareness of this loving connection.

It's vital to understand the importance of the Personal Heart Spiritual Chamber in relation to the whole. Maintaining balance in this chamber requires being present in the moment, open to taking Unconditional Love into our Personal Heart, and giving Unconditional Love to ourselves and others. As we receive Unconditional Love, it fuels the Mode of Love and allows us to share our love from a balanced Personal Heart more often.

When we develop a relationship with our Spiritual Chamber, we release control, trust in the process of life, surrender our attachment to the outcome, and recognize there is a shared responsibility for outcomes in life. The burdens in life are shared with the Source of Unconditional Love.

When we do not feel connected to the Source of Unconditional Love, our dream home can feel like something is missing. It can feel unsettled. When we feel like something is missing, it is the optimal time to become aware of what Mode we are operating from in the moment. When we operate from the Mode of Fear, it is more challenging to recognize the connection to the Source of Unconditional Love and our dream home feels less safe.

Our lower vibrational thought process dominates our perspective and, thus, our decision-making. When in the Mode of Fear in the Spiritual Chamber, it is challenging to trust love in any form—conditional or unconditional. When we shift that perception, we shift from the Mode of Fear to the Mode of Love in our Spiritual Chamber.

The Spiritual Chamber operating from the Mode of Love is in direct alignment with Unconditional Love. It does not need to control everything to create a fulfilling, love-focused life. Although Unconditional Love is our primary informant here, it does not mean we are never thrown out of balance. It means we are able to be flexible and adjust to present circumstances to maintain balance the best we can.

Unconditional Love can facilitate a connection and desire to implement more loving practices. These loving practices allow for further development and expansion in our Personal Heart Spiritual Chamber. In turn, this allows for the possibility of having more awareness of the connection to the Source of Unconditional Love in our Personal Heart Spiritual Chamber.

Further Discussion

When comparing how the Modes of Fear and Love affect each Personal Heart Chamber, it's clear they directly influence them. The Mode of Love enhances the ability of the four Personal Heart Chambers to recalibrate and rebalance. Fear does the opposite because it is focused on surviving in the short term rather than thriving in the long term.

Personal Heart Chambers do not judge situations as good or bad. Instead, they sense whether the energy is manageable and discern how to maintain balance.

When we have balance in the four Personal Heart Chambers, we function from an open Personal Heart and calm mind. Functioning this way is an ongoing practice to make the recalibration easier, more habitual, and less challenging. A dynamic relationship exists between these four Personal Heart Chambers. If one or more of these four chambers is out of balance, it can affect the other Personal Heart Chambers. They may try to overcompensate for the out-of-balance chambers and, in the process, become out of balance too.

Signs of imbalance in the four Personal Heart Chambers include being physically fatigued, experiencing emotional outbursts, energetic depletion, and lack of connection with Unconditional Love. These signs are messages for us in life to make some changes.

It's the same with our dream home. If we neglect it and cannot maintain it, things will break down. The job is more manageable if we fix it at the first signs of wear and tear. If we procrastinate or ignore the issues, they become even more problematic.

Much like our dream home, restoring balance in the four Personal Heart Chambers requires regular maintenance. Having healthy tools and practices allows us to achieve balance in the Personal Heart Chambers. You may have some beneficial practices you use now. We offer more tools and practices in Section 3.

When balance happens, we feel calm, loved, loving, heard, and seen. In balance, the Personal Heart Chambers are in alignment more frequently. Alignment increases as we gain awareness of the value of an open Personal Heart and calm mind. With more conscious awareness of the Chambers and with daily practices, we can create an open Personal Heart. It's this open Personal Heart and a calm mind that connect us to our Personal Heart Power!

CHAPTER 6

The Four Personal Heart Pillars

So far, we have explored the energies of the Personal Heart, outlined the value of awareness and consciousness in our Personal Heart, discovered the framework of the five Personal Heart States, and learned about the four Personal Heart Chambers. All of these play a significant role in the well-being of our dream home—our Personal Heart. Now we're going to take a look at the four *Personal Heart Pillars because they also play a significant role. Our **Personal Heart Pillars are the stabilizers of our Personal Heart. The four Personal Heart Pillars are Presence, Safety, Unconditional Love, and Community.**

Let's imagine our beach home is supported by four large pillars. We expect these pillars to always be there with strength and resilience, perseverance, and balance. No matter what the weather—storm or sunshine—these four large, sturdy pillars are there to protect and support our home. Our Personal Heart Pillars are meant to do the same.

Consider the foundation of our Personal Heart as the four pillars that create the level floors and structure of our home. The balance and strength of each pillar make it easy to move between the rooms—the four Personal Heart Chambers. In each room, all the items are where we like them and we find great comfort and safety in our home. At this time, everything operates as we desire.

But what happens if one pillar weakens to a point that it causes the foundation to become unlevel, and so our dream home tilts towards the compromised pillar? The pillar loses some stability, as it is weakened by stressful circumstances and struggles to hold up the weight of the home. In turn, the adjacent pillar may also struggle as it attempts to hold up more than its fair share of the weight. Eventually, the added burden of weight becomes too much and the pillars sink deeper into the ground.

The sinking pillars are one of those things that may happen gradually at first. When we notice it, we might be slightly concerned, but life is too busy to take care of it now. Time passes and life remains full. One day, while at home, the two pillars sink more dramatically into the ground and we feel the shift in our home. Sometimes, it can be so dramatic that we lose our footing and slide across the floor. Not only are we sliding, but many other things around us are moving as well. This is an abrupt change. Suddenly, our life is experiencing an upheaval, eliminating any sense of safety and causing immediate confusion and concern about what is happening to our dream home. Clearly, something is wrong.

How we react next is important. Do we quickly recalibrate from the chaos to some level of calm so we can function rationally and make the necessary decisions to move ourselves to safety quickly? Do we remain in the chaos or begin seeking solutions? How is our Mode of Operation affecting us? Do we feel alone or are there people to support us? Many factors influence the pillars of our Personal Heart and affect the stability of our dream home.

The Personal Heart Presence Pillar
The *Personal Heart Presence Pillar determines our ability to be present in the current moment. Its strength depends upon

how much we can focus on the current moment and how we can decrease distractions that pull us out of this moment. It allows things that are not relevant to our current situation to be set aside, knowing we can return to them later. When we're considering the past or future, we are pulled out of the current moment and can't fully take part in it. This can make us feel detached from this moment, which causes further challenges to being present. Becoming consciously aware of what is distracting us gives us the information needed to develop our abilities to strengthen our Presence Pillar. Therefore, practicing ways to remain present allows more opportunities to remain in an open heart and calm mind.

When we are fully present, we will ride a unicorn with butterflies and rainbows surrounding us. Just kidding! But it was a fun and playful thought. A loving Personal Heart appreciates fun and playfulness. It reminds us not to take everything so seriously.

So, when we are fully present in the moment, we can take in more information, which will mean we are better informed to make decisions that best support us. With a more supportive decision-making process, we keep the strength of this Presence Pillar strong, which helps manage the balance of the four pillars and, ultimately, the balance of our Personal Heart.

The Personal Heart Safety Pillar

The *Personal Heart Safety Pillar provides the sense of protection and well-being which is determined by our perception of any situation. The strength of this pillar is based on our thoughts, feelings, and behaviors from previous experiences, as well as our perception of the current situation. Our sense of safety varies from moment to moment and from situation to situation.

When this pillar is strong and in balance, we feel secure, believing that no harm will come to us. Each one of us may have a different sense of safety, even when we're in the same situation. These differences are important to remember because we cannot always rely on other people's perception of safety in every situation, nor can they rely on ours.

Take water, for example. As we enjoy the sea at our beach home, we feel safe swimming. We are familiar with the tides and currents because this is our home. We may be a strong swimmer, but a friend who comes to visit may not be. If we were to suggest an evening swim, they may feel concerned. Their perception of the ocean is one full of sharks and likely to be dangerous to swim in.

This is a great example of how the perception of safety determines the degree of balance within our Personal Heart Safety Pillar. In this situation, we both might think the other has an inaccurate perception. We each believe our perspective of safety is accurate. Ideally, however, we would both feel secure enough with each other to communicate our feelings and needs for safety. Communicating effectively allows us to find an activity where we both feel safe, whether or not we're in the water.

We typically feel unsafe when we're operating from the Mode of Fear. This then causes an imbalance in our Safety Pillar, making us hyper-vigilant. We figure out ways to protect ourselves. This creates a stressed and closed Personal Heart, the consequences of which mean we're less able to discern if our fear is something to respond to or whether it's something we should process through to calm ourselves down.

There is a continuum of safety in life. At one end, we feel unsafe in the present moment, and at the other, we feel completely safe. When we operate in the Mode of Fear, this unsafe feeling is prevalent. It's a perception and one that may or may not be accurate. The lower vibrational thoughts and feelings around safety can make it challenging to determine the situation accurately. To stabilize the Safety Pillar, we need to shift to the Mode of Love. And, as we're learning, this occurs when the calm mind and open Personal Heart are working optimally together. Only then can we assess the situation more accurately and do what we need to create a sense of safety.

In a balanced Personal Heart Safety Pillar, we operate from the Mode of Love; fear becomes an informant instead of a crippler. The ability to use fear as an informant allows us to understand the situation more calmly so we can take the appropriate action towards safety. With an open Personal Heart and calm mind, we can create a strong Personal Heart Safety Pillar that provides the opportunity for us to feel safe more often.

The Personal Heart Unconditional Love Pillar

The ***Personal Heart Unconditional Love Pillar is our connection to the Source of Unconditional Love. Connection to the Source gives us the ability to love ourselves and others unconditionally.** Unconditional Love is the energetic glue that connects us to our Personal Heart. It is the energy that links us to ourselves, others, and the world. The more Unconditional Love we feel for ourselves, the more our Personal Heart opens with joy, peace, and infinite Unconditional Love.

With a strong Unconditional Love Pillar, we experience love, acceptance, forgiveness, and compassion for ourselves and others. Unconditional *self-love is the major shift to a deeper Personal Heart connection and pivotal to the transition to our Personal Heart Power. When we don't feel Unconditional Love for ourselves, it is more challenging to give others Unconditional Love.

Unconditional Love does not mean we become a doormat to unhealthy behaviors. With Unconditional Love for ourselves, we can discriminate healthy relationships and situations from unhealthy ones. Creating healthy boundaries with unhealthy behaviors, other people, or stressful situations will provide the safety we need to keep our Personal Heart open. An open heart is what allows our Personal Heart Unconditional Love Pillar to become strong. When this pillar is strong, we are more likely to create healthy relationships with ourselves and others.

The Personal Heart Community Pillar

The *Personal Heart Community Pillar stabilizes our Personal Heart in relationship with others.** This Community Pillar is about the people, environments, and situations we encounter in our life. It's our Mode of Operation that determines the quality of our relationships with others and the stability of our Personal Heart Community Pillar.

The cumulation of our experiences in a community with others determines whether we approach them from the Mode of Fear or the Mode of Love. When we are rooted in fear, our sense of community is limited because our perception of what is safe in relation to others is based upon previous challenging experiences with others. Operating from the Mode of Fear in our community can be caused by one or many difficult situations or rejections. When our relationship to our Personal Heart Community Pillar is rooted in fear, our perception is skewed. This makes it more challenging for us to determine accurately if the community is safe or not.

Most of us have had a hurtful experience as a teenager when a friend in our core group betrayed us. It may have been through judgment, spreading false rumors, excluding us from a party or event, or taking our boyfriend or girlfriend away from us. As teenagers, we were less likely to have the tools to handle these types of relationship challenges, so these painful situations can leave scars on our Personal Heart. These scars remind us of how people treated us, which could create *stressful beliefs about relationships with others. **A stressful belief is a thought that carries lower vibrational energies and is incorporated into the belief system we operate from.** Such Mode of Fear stress beliefs can include:

- *People don't like me.*
- *Others can hurt me.*
- *I can't trust others.*
- *People are stupid.*

From these examples, we can recognize how it may be difficult to form healthy relationships with these beliefs. When stressful beliefs are activated, we do not want to risk being in a relationship with others because of the potential pain it could bring to us.

Stressful emotional moments affect our perception of safety within a community. Some people can forgive and learn from these challenging situations and do not carry wounds. For many, this is when the Personal Heart goes into the Mode of Fear, and they are less willing to risk being part of a community for fear of being hurt again. To feel safe in any community again requires healing old wounds and engaging healthily with others to maintain balance in our Personal Heart Community Pillar.

When we operate from the Mode of Love, our involvement in the community with others feels more safe, respectful, and connected. Fear becomes a more accurate informant. As a teenager operating from the Mode of Love, we would have been able to discern if a group is a healthy fit for us or not.

When we operate from the Mode of Love, community is important to us and we enjoy being with others. We are more willing to risk being with others and to learn from the challenging situations that can come up in relationships. We would prefer to create healthy relationships rather than stay distant from a community.

The benefit of being in a healthy community is the connection, camaraderie, support, encouragement, exchange of information, personal growth, and love. These benefits usually offset the essential pains of being in a community. When our community—whether big or small—is loving, we are fulfilled by the experiences we share. These loving experiences determine the strength of our Personal Heart Community Pillar. Having a strong community rooted in love allows for greater stability in our Personal Heart.

Further Discussion

Personal Heart Pillars can become weaker or stronger depending upon our Mode of Operation, thoughts, feelings, and behaviors. In the Mode of Fear, the lower vibrational frequencies from our thoughts, feelings, and behaviors can destabilize our pillars because they compromise the quality of energies in our Personal Heart.

In the Mode of Love, the higher vibrational frequencies from our thoughts, feelings, and behaviors can enhance the stabilization of the four Personal Heart Pillars. The Pillars do not judge situations as good or bad. Instead, they sense whether energy is manageable or unmanageable. The stabilization occurs because the quality of the higher vibrational energies is enhanced in our Personal Heart. This contributes to a calm mind and an open heart. Being consciously aware of these Personal Heart Pillars allows us to make choices to transition to higher vibrational energies within our heart.

The Personal Heart Pillars and Chambers are separate aspects of the Personal Heart, yet they operate interdependently. The four Chambers provide internal support to our Personal Heart, while the four Pillars provide external support to it. As the Chambers bring the Personal Heart internal peace, so the Pillars bring external stabilization. As one ebbs and flows, so does the other.

When the pillars and chambers function optimally together, we have a strong and balanced foundation for the Personal Heart—our beach home. In turn, the stabilization of our Personal Heart Pillars provides a level foundation for the Personal Heart Chambers. This provides the optimal environment for the Personal Heart Chambers to remain balanced.

When our Mode of Operation is Fear, one or more of our Personal Heart Pillars and Chambers are challenged and we can lose balance in our Personal Heart. Our overall functioning becomes short-sighted, with a decreased awareness of higher vibrational thoughts, feelings, and behaviors. Our mind becomes stressed and our Personal Heart closes, limiting their connection and our ability to use Personal Heart Power.

Conversely, when our Mode of Operation is Love, we have strong support from the four balanced Personal Heart Pillars and Chamber, so our Personal Heart operates optimally. Just like in our beach home, we can function effectively with our Personal Heart Power.

The interconnectedness and the effects of the Personal Heart Chambers, Pillars, States, and the Modes of Operation influence our functioning within the Personal Heart. The four *Personal Heart Functions are the next layer of our Personal Heart Power framework.

CHAPTER 7

The Four Personal Heart Functions

As the vibrational frequencies of our Personal Heart affect the Personal Heart Chambers, Pillars, and States, they also affect our Personal Heart Functions. **Personal Heart Functions are the way energy is managed within the Personal Heart. There are four Personal Heart Functions: Taking, Dismissing, Giving, and Withholding.**

We live in an ocean of energy that creates vibrational frequencies that surround a particular experience. Vibrational energy surrounds us at every moment. Consciously or unconsciously, we take in, dismiss, give out, or withhold the vibrational energy from which we function. The energetic quality of the function depends on—you guessed it—the Mode of Operation: Fear or Love.

In our ocean of energy, several vibrational energies are operating both inside and outside our Personal Heart. The external energies come from various sources such as the Source of Unconditional Love, other people, nature, animals, physical surroundings, and frankly, on some level, anything that exists. The internal energy arises from our thoughts, feelings, behaviors, and the Source of Unconditional Love. All of life has vibrational energy, whether or not we are aware of sensing it.

The Personal Heart has developed an energy filtering system within itself to manage the ocean of external energy entering it. This begins with receiving energy through our senses. Our Personal Heart then uses our present Mode of Operation to filter which feelings we choose to send to our mind for interpretation. This filtering occurs subconsciously or consciously.

Our awareness, training, and practice with all of our senses determine our ability to accurately or completely understand situations. Our primary focus of perceiving energies through the mind and not the Personal Heart may limit our perception of the sensory information we are receiving. When we function only through the mind, our insight is compromised because it is not acknowledging the information from the heart. This limits our Personal Heart functioning at a greater capacity. Remember, our optimal Personal Heart Power comes when we have union with a calm mind and an open Personal Heart.

To receive the most accurate, comprehensive, and beneficial vibrational energies, our Personal Heart is functioning from the Mode of Love. Having the desire to function from the Mode of Love moves us towards greater consciousness and a higher vibrational functioning each day. It is an unrealistic expectation of ourselves and others to function constantly from the Mode of Love. But it is realistic to have a desire to live from the Mode of Love more often each day.

Being aware of our Personal Heart State shows us from which mode we are operating and how we will receive the vibrational energies that surround us. We receive energetic information every moment of the day. By learning more about the four Personal Heart Functions, our awareness of how we can manage the energies flowing in and out of our Personal Heart will improve. And, with more awareness, we can better manage the functioning of our Personal Heart.

On an energetic level, each Personal Heart Function has a specific action to manage the energy it receives from our feelings—the sensing information being processed in our Personal Heart. Each Personal Heart Function filters vibrational energy for the Personal Heart and has a slightly different role in managing the energy flow. The operation and management of these energies in the Personal Heart Functions are in relation to oneself, others, and the world. Let's look at each of the Personal Heart Functions in turn.

The ***Personal Heart Taking Function manages the quality and quantity of the vibrational energies we take into our Personal Heart.** These are the energies we allow in.

The ***Personal Heart Dismissing Function prevents vibrational energies from coming into our Personal Heart.** These are the energies we don't let in.

The ***Personal Heart Giving Function sends vibrational energies out from the Personal Heart.** These are the energies we give out.

The ***Personal Heart Withholding Function suppresses vibrational energies from being given out from the Personal Heart.** These are the energies we hold back.

These four Personal Heart Functions work together to manage efficient flows of energy into and out of our Personal Heart. When they are not working together, it causes disruption in the higher vibrational energy flow. Management from the Mode of Love maintains balance and function with our Personal Heart Power.

The Relationship between the Personal Heart Taking and Dismissing Functions

The four Personal Heart Functions activate as we make choices. Choices trigger a potential energy shift. These shifts determine how we manage the energies we receive or sense within our Personal Heart. As we sense and filter the vibrational energies of feelings coming into our Personal Heart, the Taking and Dismissing Functions are activated.

Processing feelings can quickly become complicated and confusing, especially when we consider what David DiSalvo wrote in his article, *Your Brain Sees Even When You Don't*: "The unconscious processing abilities of the human brain are estimated at roughly 11 million pieces of information per second. Compare that to the estimate for conscious processing: about 40 pieces per second."[13] This article continues that even though we cannot process all those bits of information consciously, they still can affect our lives.

Just stop for a moment and look at what is around you. Imagine how many bits of information you are receiving unconsciously, just in your visual surroundings. Now add all your other senses. It's easy to realize how that information rises to eleven million bits so quickly.

Fascinating, isn't it? As DiSalvo stated, we can only consciously receive about forty bits of information per second. That big difference explains why we often feel confused and overwhelmed with life and our experiences. Being aware of this information offers more understanding of the complexity of receiving vibrational energetic information. In turn, we can consciously decide what energy to take into our Personal Heart and what energy to dismiss.

Our activated Mode of Operation will set up the vibrational filter within the Personal Heart of what it will take in or dismiss. If the Mode of Fear is activated, the Taking Function takes in the external lower vibrational energies, such as anger, sadness, and fear, into the Personal Heart. At the same time, the Dismissing Function is activated to dismiss the higher vibrational energies. In the Mode of Fear, the Personal Heart struggles to take in feelings of Unconditional Love, joy, or peace because these are higher vibrational feelings that are challenging to take in by the Mode of Fear due to the vibrational differences. Our Personal Heart will dismiss these higher vibrational feelings even when they may be more beneficial for us. Knowing this allows us to recognize the benefit of conscious awareness when making choices about what energies we will take in or dismiss.

On the other hand, if the Personal Heart is in the Mode of Love, the Taking Function allows feelings such as Unconditional Love, joy, and peace to be taken in. In this Mode, the Dismissing Function recognizes choices when lower vibrational feelings show up. In the discerning process of choice, the lower vibrational feelings are either dismissed easily or are processed through until they can be dismissed.

Our Personal Heart usually senses the internal and external energies and then takes in what supports our currently activated Mode of Operation and dismisses what doesn't support it. This typically occurs unconsciously. Becoming more conscious of the inflow of energy allows us to make choices about what energy we want to take into or dismiss from our Personal Heart.

We can consciously shift our Mode of Operation from Fear to Love by shifting the vibrational quality of our thoughts, feelings, and behaviors. This is why so many of us appreciate quotes and affirmations that support higher vibrational energies. In the Mode of Fear, these higher vibrational quotes can be irritating rather than supportive. This is because the vibrational frequency is higher than the Personal Heart can take in at its current state.

For each moment when energy is flowing into our Personal Heart, we can respond proactively or impulsively to shift the energy. With conscious awareness, we are aware if we are functioning from the Mode of Fear or Love. When functioning habitually, we let in the vibrational energy flow that supports our Mode of Operation, based on previous experiences.

Transitioning between the Modes of Fear and Love is usually because of perceptions in the Personal Heart and mind. For example, if our Personal Heart and mind perceive any of the following: we're unsafe, don't feel lovable, or do not have enough of something in the moment, our Personal Heart can automatically go into the Mode of Fear. If we perceive in our Personal Heart and mind that we are safe in the moment, feel lovable, and have enough of whatever, then our Personal Heart shifts more easily to the Mode of Love.

In addition to taking in our internal energies in our Personal Heart, we also take in external vibrational energies from outside sources, including from other people and our environment. This also can happen on a conscious or unconscious level.

If we think back to our story of the mother coming to visit her daughter's new home, it showed how the daughter was taking in her mother's comments from the Mode of Fear. She felt judgment from her mother. At the same time, the mother chose to dismiss the daughter's lower vibrational judgment. Instead of reacting and taking in the external vibrations from her daughter, the mother dismissed her daughter's comments and suggested they step inside the new home, allowing for a shift to more love.

It is usually easier to take in higher vibrational energies from other people's feelings and behaviors because this typically gives us more support for the Mode of Love in our Personal Heart. Many of us naturally feel safe and enjoy being around higher vibrational people when we are in the Mode of Love. Sometimes we even feel their higher vibrational energy as it supports our shift from the Mode of Fear into the Mode of Love. This is commonly called *lifting your spirits* because we feel better being around them.

Higher vibrational people tend to create higher vibrational environments that feel safe and fun to be in. It is easier to keep our Personal Heart open for taking in this higher vibrational energy from others. However, if we are in a Disconnected Personal Heart State with the Mode of Fear activated, the higher vibrational energies can be more challenging, so we dismiss it. It's like turning on a dazzling white light in a dark room. Fortunately, we can create opportunities to shift our Personal Heart State and Mode of Operation to restore balance. There are specific tools in Section 3 that will support you with this.

Another challenge arises when we take in lower vibrational energies from other people's feelings and behaviors, especially if our own Personal Heart is in the Mode of Love at that time. Their lower vibrational energies can influence a potential shift from the Mode of Love to the Mode of Fear in our Personal Heart. This is why conscious awareness is *so* important. When people are functioning from lower vibrational energies, they tend to create lower vibrational environments that don't feel safe or fun to be in. Therefore, it is important to set healthy boundaries for what we take into our Personal Heart from external energy sources.

We have the conscious ability to limit what energy we take in from other people, as well as from our own thoughts. A healthy boundary can be as simple as dismissing what others say or do in the moment. It is also about changing our own negative self-talk. When we realize how the type of energy we take in matters, we make higher vibrational choices more often and more consistently. We can set a stronger boundary if we have the courage to have a conversation to work through the challenging situation. We can't control others, but we can control ourselves. We can state what we need, change our thoughts, and choose our responses so we can stay in balance in our Personal Heart, even when the other person is not in balance. Just like us, the other person will choose to respond depending upon their Mode of Operation. With conscious awareness, we are more likely to recognize how our Mode of Operation is functioning in relation to the other person. We can also assess the situation more accurately. This allows for healthier boundaries as needed.

If those boundaries aren't effective enough, we can choose to limit our time being around that person and their lower vibrational energies. Remember, *we can't change anyone else's thoughts, feelings, or behaviors.* We can choose whether we will take in or dismiss the energies presented to us. This is our Personal Heart Power.

The Personal Heart Taking Function brings in the energy the Personal Heart needs or desires, depending on our Mode of Operation and Personal Heart State. The Dismissing Function will not let in the energy the Personal Heart does not desire, cannot take in, or is not beneficial in the moment.

The quantity of the higher and lower vibrational energy being taken in or dismissed from our Personal Hearts can matter as much as the quality does. If the quantities of energies coming in are too overwhelming, we can dismiss them. There are a variety of ways and reasons we might choose to do this. We dismiss energies that feel overwhelming and only take in what feels familiar in our current Mode of Operation. When we desire a more love-focused life, we can consciously choose to take in higher vibrational energies that are manageable and needed for optimal Personal Heart functioning.

Even if we want more Unconditional Love in our life, we can quickly become overwhelmed by it if we are in the Mode of Fear, should a generous amount of it come our way. Have you ever had someone who showered you with too much kindness? Instead of accepting it with joy and appreciation, did you become suspicious of their actions and motives? This is an example of being overwhelmed with higher vibrational energies from someone else. It may cause us to dismiss this Unconditional Love because we cannot take it in at that moment. For this reason, it is important to feel compassion, patience, and understanding without judgment about how we currently operate in our Personal Heart. These compassionate feelings can become the drivers for our Personal Heart expansion. In addition, being aware of this allows us to recognize when we are taking in or dismissing higher vibrational energies. It allows us to make different choices and to use tools and practices for more effective and efficient heart functioning.

The more open our Personal Heart, the higher vibrational energy it can take in for optimal functioning. Our open Personal

Heart allows us to feel a greater vibrational range of feelings and to determine the quantity and quality of them in relation to our Personal Heart. This ability empowers us with greater expertise to choose which energies to take in and which to dismiss to remain in balance in our Personal Heart.

Not only can we discern the benefits of taking in higher vibrational energies, but we can also determine the risk of lower vibrational energies. When we recognize these risks, we can dismiss what does not benefit our Personal Heart Power. The practice we put into understanding and balancing our Personal Heart in the Personal Heart Chambers, Pillars, and Functions allows us to feel a wide vibrational range of feelings without getting out of balance. So, becoming more aware of the Personal Heart's Taking and Dismissing Functions allows us to make healthier choices regarding what we take in and dismiss from our Personal Heart. This, too, supports our Personal Heart Power.

The Relationship between the Personal Heart Giving and Withholding Functions

While the Personal Heart Taking and Dismissing Functions filter the energies coming into our heart, the Personal Heart Giving and Withholding Functions filter the energies going out.

The Giving Function manages the energy coming out of our Personal Heart. The energy we give to ourselves, and others, will influence the quality of our relationships with ourselves and others. When we give out too much or too little from our Personal Heart, we will feel an imbalance in it.

Using the Personal Heart Giving Function can happen on a conscious or unconscious level. The energy coming out of our Personal Heart depends on our Mode of Operation. If we're operating from the Mode of Fear, we will give lower vibrational thoughts, feelings, and behaviors to ourselves and others.

For example, at the party scenario with the hors d'oeuvres, the hostess thought her friend did not like them, causing her to feel judged by her friend. Her lower vibrational response to her friend was a reaction to her perceived judgment, which determined her response. When our perception is energized from fear, we tend to give out the same. This can become a pattern of behavior of giving ourselves, as well as others, lower vibrational energy rooted in fear. This won't enhance a healthy relationship with others. People can sense, on some energetic level, when we are not giving them what they want or need to sustain a healthy relationship. To get out of this pattern, we need to shift toward the Mode of Love.

When we operate from the Mode of Love in our Personal Heart, the self-love feelings will give out higher vibrational energy to support our higher vibrational thoughts, feelings, and behaviors. Overall, we feel good about being ourselves. This becomes a higher vibrational feedback loop that affects what we give to ourselves and out to others. Going back to the party scenario, if she had perceived her friend's comment as a compliment, she would have been able to give out a higher vibrational response. We can freely give from our Personal Heart only what we already have in our heart.

When we are in the Mode of Love, then we are giving others higher vibrational thoughts, feelings, and behaviors that can enhance healthy relationships. For example, if we can give a loving compliment to someone else, the higher vibrational energies of our compliment are more likely to enhance our relationship with them. It's our Mode of Operation, our Personal Heart State, and our quality of functioning that will determine our ability to give lower or higher vibrational energy in any situation.

When we're consciously aware of the Personal Heart Giving Function, it allows us to know when we can give higher vibrational energies to ourselves and others, while still staying in balance with an open Personal Heart and calm mind. Conversely, if we're unconscious of our Personal Heart Giving Function, then we can't consciously manage the energy coming from our Personal Heart. Therefore, sometimes we can say or do things that might hurt other people without realizing what vibrational energy we were giving out in the moment. However, giving out lower vibrational energy can also be done intentionally. This intentional lower vibrational functioning of our Personal Heart Giving Function can hinder our ability to have healthy relationships with others. Knowing that the energy we give out influences the quality of our relationships with ourselves and others enables us to determine what we need to give and how we will choose to give it. When we choose not to give out energies, we are withholding.

The Personal Heart Withholding Function controls the quality and quantity of energy we hold back from ourselves, others, and the world. As with all the Personal Heart Functions, this process often happens unconsciously, but we can decide consciously what energy we want to withhold. The activated Mode of Operation also sets the vibrational filters in the Personal Heart Withholding Function.

When we're operating from the Mode of Fear, we act from feelings of survival and scarcity—we perceive there is not enough of something. The Personal Heart Withholding Function limits what we share from our Personal Heart. This might be through a sense of scarcity, whereby we believe that if we give it to others, then we will not have enough left for ourselves. For example, if we withhold compassion toward ourselves, we will probably withhold compassion for others. We can also withhold patience, forgiveness, love, acceptance, and other resources from ourselves and others when we believe there is not enough to go around.

We may also fear being judged and rejected by others, so we withhold from sharing our authentic self. These fear perceptions for withholding lead to more fear and keep us stuck in the Mode of Fear.

On the other hand, if our Personal Heart is in the Mode of Love, we are in the thriving and abundance mode. We believe in an abundance of love and other higher vibrational energy feelings and that we can share them with others and still stay in balance. The Personal Heart Withholding Function provides the check and balance of the Personal Heart. If we fall out of balance with energy, stamina, time, or other resources, we might decide to withhold sharing these resources to stay in balance.

Imagine, for example, that you have given your best effort and time to help a friend move into her new apartment. After hours of helping her, you begin to feel tired. You let your friend know you need to leave and get some rest. Your friend understands and appreciates your help. This is a form of self-care. You gave all that you could for the day—the capacity you have left; you withhold for yourself to stay in balance.

If instead of appreciating your help, your friend makes an off comment about you having a lack of commitment to the move, you can then choose to withhold your judgmental comments. You accept that she does not understand why you are leaving. After all, she too is tired. And the reason you understand this is because you have not allowed yourself to get out of balance and slip into the Mode of Fear. You can empathize with her being out of balance with the stress of moving.

Being able to withhold lower vibrational energy from others in the Mode of Love means we keep our judgmental thoughts to ourselves. In this instance, the Personal Heart Withholding Function in the Mode of Love keeps us in higher vibrational energy and balance. If we want to live from our Personal Heart Power, we need to be mindful of how we respond to and share energies with our circle of people.

The Personal Heart Giving and Withholding Functions guide how we use and share our energies with ourselves and others. When in the Mode of Fear, this functioning can feel challenging and confusing as we give and withhold from a lower vibrational Personal Heart State. The opposite is true when in the Mode of Love, where we function from a higher vibrational Personal Heart State. A higher vibrational state gives us the ability to discern what we can give or need to withhold in any situation and still stay in balance. We will feel our best when the four Personal Heart Functions co-operate and work together to keep the Personal Heart open, in balance, and operating from the Mode of Love.

Becoming more conscious of the Personal Heart Functions—Taking, Dismissing, Giving, and Withholding—gives us the power to make healthier choices to stay in balance. Effectively functioning from the Mode of Love develops the ability for our Personal Heart to remain in balance more frequently. This balance allows for a greater possibility to connect it with our calm mind, and this enables us to operate and function from the higher vibrational Personal Heart States. This is when we can function from our Personal Heart Power and live a love-focused life!

CHAPTER 8

Deeper with the Five Personal Heart States

Understanding the interconnection between the two Modes of Operation, the four Personal Heart Chambers, Pillars, and Functions, and how they affect the five Personal Heart States is when we really begin to tap into our Personal Heart Power. So, let's look deeper into how the weaving and interaction of all these different aspects of our Personal Heart determine our Personal Heart State.

The Disconnected Personal Heart State

In this heart state:

- Our mind is in the Mode of Fear, making us believe we have limited or no choices.
- The Personal Heart is closed, and the mind is stressed and chaotic because they are functionally disconnected from each other and operating independently.

- The range of experience tends to be on a continuum from numbness to extreme overwhelm.
- Thoughts often get stuck in Stress Loops of past or future scenarios extinguishing the present moment.
- Feelings tend to be totally shut down or too intense to tolerate due to our inability to process through our feelings with a chaotic mind.
- Behaviors are in survival mode, which drives us into the fight, flight, or freeze behaviors.

Let's imagine our beach home is in a dilapidated and non-functioning state. There has been an obvious lack of attention given to it. Imagine the four pillars have been weakened to the point of collapse. The foundations are failing—unable to support the home. The Safety Pillar has been greatly compromised or nonexistent. It's now difficult to determine where the rooms used to be, not to mention where all the household items belong. To top it off, there is no electricity, water, or any other services. Looking at it feels uninviting, overwhelming, and unsafe. This home needs a complete renovation from top to bottom. Where do we even begin?

Like the beach home, our Personal Heart in the Disconnected State operates miserably. There has been an obvious lack of attention to the Personal Heart Chambers from the mind as it functions in survival mode. The four Personal Heart Pillars are struggling to maintain strength to support the Personal Heart. We are completely in the Mode of Fear in this Personal Heart State.

In this heart state, the Presence Pillar—the ability to stay in the moment and perceive the situation accurately—is difficult. We're already stuck in the Stress Loops about the past or future challenging situations and ignore the feelings of the Personal Heart in the present moment.

In the Disconnected State, the Mode of Fear dominates, severely compromising the Safety Pillar. The mind functions alone and assesses the situation only from fear. The Mode of Fear uses the perception of past experiences for predicting the future. It feels unsafe in virtually every situation because of the belief that life is happening to you rather than for you.

The Unconditional Love Pillar is perceived to be completely disconnected from the Personal Heart and mind. If love exists at all, it is conditional. If love is offered, we believe it's because there is an expectation that something is required in return. In this state, it is not possible to recognize when Unconditional Love is truly being offered unconditionally. If love is perceived in this state, our mindset doesn't trust the love and wonders, *What is the catch?*

In this Personal Heart State, we can feel isolated and alone. This makes it difficult to recognize the Community Pillar, even when we are in a group of people. The disconnected heart, in relationship to the Community Pillar, perceives no support from others and reciprocates by giving no support to others. This makes it nearly inconceivable to form healthy relationships.

In the Disconnected Heart State, the relationship between the Personal Heart and the four Personal Heart Chambers is internally unbalanced, creating an inability to work effectively with the mind. Ideally, the four Personal Heart Chambers work together within the Personal Heart to keep it in balance. In the Disconnected Heart State, balance cannot be achieved because of the magnitude of lower vibrational energies.

Fear energy can only support lower vibrational functioning within the Personal Heart Chambers. This makes it nearly impossible to find balance among those chambers. The Energetic Chamber is operating from the Mode of Fear, thus emitting lower vibrational energy for functioning. The Mode of Fear activates the fight, flight, or freeze reaction. This causes the Physical Chamber to be managed by the sympathetic nervous system, causing symptoms of physical stress. The Sensing Chamber feels lower vibrational feelings—if it feels at all.

In the Spiritual Chamber, it is highly unlikely to perceive or feel a connection to the Source of Unconditional Love.

The Personal Heart cannot function well when the mind struggles with internal stressful and chaotic thoughts. This struggle makes it challenging for the Personal Heart and mind to connect, keeping them isolated from one another. The information we are receiving can be sensed differently by the Personal Heart and mind. This is when internal conflict occurs—our heart is telling us one thing while our mind is telling us another. For both the Personal Heart and the mind, this is a painful, lonely, and seemingly insurmountable Personal Heart State. When we're in this state, we need courage to seek outside support until we find what we need to connect to our Personal Heart. We are worth the effort.

If we encounter people in a Disconnected Personal Heart State, offer them compassion when possible, not judgment. We may give them the glimmer of hope they need to seek the necessary support to connect to their Personal Heart. It is important to avoid becoming the rescuer because we believe it is our responsibility to make them happy. Being around others in a compassionate and loving way requires healthy functioning in our own Personal Heart.

The Reactive Personal Heart State

In this heart state:

- Our Mode of Operation is Fear and choices appear limited with conditional love as an informant.
- The Personal Heart is mainly closed. Stressful situations are ruminating in our mind.
- The range of experience tends to be on a continuum, from overwhelmed to stressful.
- Thoughts are typically lower vibrational and are predominantly about the past or future.

- Stressful beliefs of self and others, and Stress Loops are commonplace.
- Feelings tend to be of a heightened sensitivity, out of balance to the situation, and predominantly lower vibrational. However, we are beginning to sense our feelings. We may not like them, but we are sensing them.
- We tend to take things personally, even when things are not about us.
- We make decisions for short-term gain versus long-term balance.
- Behavior is reactive and focused on short-term gain rather than long-term balance.

Now let's imagine the beach home again. The beach home is in disarray and in a minimally functioning state. It has been ignored for quite some time. The four Personal Heart Pillars have been weakened and are shaky, but they are still standing. This creates an unstable foundation compromising the structure of the home. The rooms are there but in precarious conditions. Household items are messy and in a jumbled way.

When the light is switched on, it immediately dims and has inconsistent power. This causes frustration. We doubt the other services will work well. Further exploration around the home triggers more feelings of uncertainty and disappointment. Surely the house should have been in a better condition than this. This home needs major remodeling, including structural work. Our Personal Heart is not functioning well.

There is only a minimal connection between the Personal Heart and mind. This fragile connection creates challenges in making clear and healthy decisions because of fear. The Mode of Fear can create confusion and chaos.

The four Personal Heart Pillars begin to gain some strength, although they still cannot consistently support the Personal Heart. The strength of the Personal Heart Pillars is often compromised because of the lack of connection between the heart and mind. In the Reactive Personal Heart State, the ability of the mind to recognize the support from the Personal Heart Pillars is difficult. Then, when it is recognized, it is usually not trusted.

We still find the Personal Heart Presence Pillar—the ability to stay in the present moment—difficult. Past and future thoughts still dominate. The Mode of Fear dominates, compromising the Personal Heart Safety Pillar. The mind still functions primarily alone and assesses the situation, primarily from fear. Fear still assesses the situation based on past experiences or future possibilities in relation to the past. It feels unsafe in many situations because of the limited communication and connection between the Personal Heart and mind.

The Unconditional Love Pillar fills with conditional love from the mind. The mind then controls the quantity and quality of love in this Personal Heart State. This creates the belief, and the expectation, that something is required in return for love. In this Reactive Personal Heart State, conditional love may be recognized, whereas Unconditional Love is not. Conditional love may be present in this heart state. The mindset is prepared to react.

In this state, we may feel a sense of community with others who have similar beliefs. The Reactive Personal Heart, in relation to the Community Pillar, has a perception of conditional support *from* and *for* others. Relationships are conditional, based on our perception of whether someone is with us or against us.

The relationship of the Personal Heart with the four Personal Heart Chambers to move into any sense of balance is challenged internally. In this state, the Personal Heart and mind conflict with one another or are working together in fear. The balance in the chambers remains challenging because of the lower vibration of the fear energy. The Mode of Fear can only support lower vibrational functioning within the Personal Heart Chambers.

With conditional love entering the Reactive Personal Heart State, the extent of the fight, flight, or freeze reaction is lessened compared with the Disconnected Personal Heart State, yet it is still more than the Half-hearted Heart State.

The Energetic Chamber operates from the Mode of Fear with conditional love as an informant. The sympathetic nervous system is still activating stressful physical symptoms, but not to the extreme of the disconnected heart.

The Sensing Chamber primarily feels lower vibrational feelings. Although feelings may rise in this Personal Heart State, they may either be suppressed or overreactive. The feelings keep building and building until they cannot be suppressed any longer and they become overreactive.

The Physical Chamber is either pushing itself to its limits or it is inactive. Over time, these extremes are what contribute to imbalance as well as health issues. This includes mental and physical health.

The Spiritual Chamber has a limited perception of a connection to the Source of Unconditional Love, if it exists at all in this state.

With a stressful mind in the Reactive Personal Heart State, a healthy connection between the Personal Heart and mind becomes challenging because at least one of them, and often both, are reactive. The triggers from past emotional pain that have been stored rather than processed through affect our emotions. The overly emotional reaction might have little to do with the current situation. People in the Reactive Personal Heart State need compassion and love from others instead of judgment, but don't we all?

The Half-Hearted Personal Heart State

In this heart state:

- Our Mode of Operation fluctuates between Fear and Love.
- The Personal Heart fluctuates between being open and closed, and the mind fluctuates between being calm and overthinking. The Personal Heart and mind begin to work together more consistently in the Mode of Love.
- The range of experiences tends to be on a continuum, from less stressful to somewhat manageable, often swinging like a pendulum in the current situation.
- Thoughts fluctuate between *life is half-empty*, and *life is half-full*, inspiring the desire for life to become different. Stress Loops can be triggered and continue to show up during the *half-empty* perceptions.
- Feelings may swing from being in balance to out of balance, but not as dramatically as in the Reactive Heart State. We alternate between lower and higher vibrational feelings, making situations less stressful than the Reactive Heart State, although not yet optimal.
- Perception of having choices shifts depending upon your Mode of Operation.
- Behavior is based on the Mode of Operation in the present moment. In the Mode of Fear, behavior is reactive. In the Mode of Love, the opportunity exists to choose healthier behaviors for more balance and optimal outcomes.
- This is the Personal Heart State where you can begin to connect to your Personal Heart Power.

Let's go back to our beach home again. In this state, at first glance, it looks promising and functional. It has been somewhat maintained and looks fairly good. The four Personal Heart Pillars are relatively stable, although some of them could use some maintenance. They're providing a stable foundation, but the structure could be compromised if the maintenance is not tended to.

The rooms are clearly defined and have potential. The household items are fine and somewhat organized. Turning on the light, it's reassuring to see it functions, but it seems a little dim. It could be brighter. What about the water and other services? Are they more reliable than the lights? Maybe they are. Maybe they aren't. Generally, the home triggers both feelings of hope and uncertainty. Overall, it is in a fair condition even if it needs some repair and some minor structural work. This is a project that feels more manageable to take on if you are up to the task.

In the Half-hearted Personal Heart State, our Personal Heart functions fairly well. The connection between the heart and mind can fluctuate between working in harmony and being in some degree of conflict. Sometimes the mind is easily distracted and operates without the Personal Heart, other times it is calm and operating with it.

The four Personal Heart Pillars are offering moderate stability. If the required maintenance is not done on a specific pillar, it could become unstable and cause a compromise to the stability of the Personal Heart foundation. The Personal Heart Pillars' strength increases and decreases depending upon the ability to recognize when one or more pillars are being compromised. The strength of a pillar increases when we choose and take action to strengthen it. The pillars may decrease in strength when they are not cared for. Consciously recognizing the support of the Personal Heart Pillars often creates a healthier engagement in life. This healthier engagement allows us to make choices to strengthen our pillars to maintain stability in our Personal Heart.

In this heart state, the Personal Heart Presence Pillar fluctuates between being present in the moment and being distracted. Sometimes the past and future thoughts can still preoccupy our mind. Consciousness is more prevalent, which means it's possible to use our awareness to make more beneficial choices in the present moment.

The Safety Pillar can fluctuate on the continuum of stability to instability because our Mode of Operation shifts between Fear and Love. The mind and the Personal Heart work together in the Mode of Love, which allows communication to flow freely between them, giving a greater sense of safety. In the Mode of Fear, the Personal Heart and stressful mind have challenges communicating. It is more of a push-and-pull versus a flow, which weakens the sense of safety.

As Unconditional Love enters the Personal Heart, the Unconditional Love Pillar strengthens and becomes more stable. Its stability fluctuates depending upon whether the Mode of Fear or Love currently energizes the Personal Heart. The quality of the vibrational energy determines the Personal Heart capacity of how much Unconditional Love we can take into our heart and how much Unconditional Love we can give out. Awareness of taking in and giving out Unconditional Love begins in this Half-hearted Personal Heart State.

In this Personal Heart State, the perception of community is broadening. We recognize that, within our different communities, we have a different level of comfort or connection to the people. Regarding the Personal Heart Community Pillar, the Half-hearted State recognizes more support in some communities and less support in others. Relationships are becoming healthier, more supportive, and more reciprocal.

In the Half-hearted State, the relationship of the Personal Heart with the four Personal Heart Chambers has the potential to achieve a sense of balance. In the Mode of Love, the Personal Heart and mind are working together. The sense of balance is achievable, albeit challenging at times. The vibrational fluctuations of the feelings in this state are less extreme and stressful in the four Personal Heart Chambers.

In the Energetic Chamber, the continuum of energy ebbs and flows depending upon your Mode of Operation. In the Physical Chamber, we make healthier choices more often because we can recognize the benefits of creating physical balance. In the Sensing Chamber, we begin to become more aware of how the lower and higher vibrational frequencies influence our feelings. The Spiritual Chamber is more accepting of love and there is the potential of Unconditional Love being taken in and given out.

In this state, we recognize there is the possibility of better functioning with more balance in our life. This recognition motivates us to make healthier choices that allow us to operate from the Mode of Love more often, which supports a shift to the Content Heart State.

The Content Personal Heart State

In this state:
- Our Mode of Operation is Love.
- The Personal Heart is primarily open, the mind is essentially calm, and they are functioning in nearly full alignment, rooted in love. This is Personal Heart Power.
- The range of experience tends to be on a continuum, from manageable to fulfilled.
- Thoughts can remain in the present moment and we believe life is on our side. If a Stress Loop presents itself, we process through it effectively.
- Feelings are primarily higher vibrational, with a sense of peace and belief that life will work out. We can primarily manage and process through feelings effectively to maintain balanced feelings.
- We're aware of an abundance of choices, and we intend to make them wise choices rooted in Unconditional Love. Our beliefs are more reassuring and less attached to outcomes.

- Healthier behaviors are chosen to achieve or maintain balance in the various aspects of the Personal Heart.

This time, the beach home looks beautiful and inviting. It has been well-maintained and cared for. The four pillars are stable, offering sufficient support to the home. The rooms are exquisite, with nearly everything well organized and in its place. Switching on the lights, they work as expected and light up the beautiful space. Naturally, the water and other services also work properly. Looking around the home generates feelings of contentment, coziness, and security. This home is what you have been looking for and you are excited to own it, maintain it, and live in it! You feel overjoyed!

In the Content Personal Heart State, our Personal Heart feels joyful. We function optimally and feel full of Unconditional Love much of the time. We are aware the Source of Unconditional Love is there for us all the time, even though we may not always feel connected to it.

The connection between the Personal Heart and calm mind has developed into a well-balanced relationship rooted in Unconditional Love. We feel grateful for the calm mind working together as a willing and loving partner with our Personal Heart. Our Mode of Operation is Love—fear informs us for the most favorable functioning in our life. In the Content Personal Heart State, we can consciously recognize our Personal Heart Power and the opportunities to use it.

The four Personal Heart Pillars are stable and well-balanced. The ongoing maintenance needed for each one happens regularly. There is no desire to compromise the stability of our Personal Heart Power. We fully recognize that the support of the four Personal Heart Pillars is important to our overall well-being in life.

In the Personal Heart Presence Pillar, the ability to stay in the moment is routine because the mind is present more of the time.

Processing through feelings effectively or enjoying them in this Personal Heart State is part of the process. We know the rewards of processing through our lower vibrational feelings and do what is needed to rebalance with higher vibrational feelings. Here, we maintain higher vibrational energy and it feels too good to compromise it.

In the Content Personal Heart State, we have a strong Personal Heart Safety Pillar because we're operating from the Mode of Love with fear as our informant. We know we have the power to create safety in our life. We do this internally by setting healthy limits with our thoughts, feelings, and behaviors, and externally by setting healthy boundaries and limits with others. As the mind and Personal Heart work together in the Mode of Love, the communication between them flows freely. This creates a strong sense of safety and thus a stable pillar. We specifically know what we need to continue to keep ourselves safe.

As Love has become the Mode of Operation, the Personal Heart Unconditional Love Pillar is solid. This higher vibrational energy means our Personal Heart capacity is optimal. The stability of this pillar means we typically take in and give out Unconditional Love to ourselves and others. It also means we can recognize when others are giving conditional love, and so we can consciously decide if we want to take that in or dismiss it.

The Community Pillar in this state is when we perceive our community with a heartwarming, healthy, and supportive connection. Individual and community feelings and needs are respected and supported. Functioning in this state is good for us as well as good for the whole. We know we can choose what communities we desire to be connected to.

We choose communities that offer healthy environments and relationships as much as possible. When we find ourselves in a community that does not offer contentment, we remove ourselves from it or work to change it. We know that within the different communities, people affect us, and we affect other people. In relationship to the Community Pillar, the Content Personal Heart State perceives support within our communities. Relationships are healthy and support is reciprocal. It feels good to be a part of such communities. We feel a sense of belonging to something greater than ourselves, and we are happy and grateful for being a part of it.

In the Content Personal Heart State, the relationship between the four Personal Heart Chambers is typically balanced when they are individually balanced. In the Personal Heart Energetic Chamber, we are rooted in the Mode of Love and function with the Source of Unconditional Love. We use fear as an informant. In the Physical Chamber, we know how to stabilize and maintain the various components of physical balance. The Sensing Chamber can maintain the higher vibrations more effectively and more consistently. When lower vibrational feelings present themselves, we process through them intentionally and consciously to restore emotional balance. The Spiritual Chamber maintains connections to the Source of Unconditional Love and we have an awareness of this connection.

In this state, we have reassuring beliefs about ourselves and others. We recognize that others, like us, are trying to figure out how to navigate this life. It eases the temptation to judge or take things personally. We are well-balanced and can primarily go with the flow of life.

In this heart state, we have a conscious relationship with our Personal Heart. We function with awareness in our decision-making process for the optimal relationship between the Personal Heart and calm mind. This awareness also allows us to recognize others' differing Personal Heart States, which mitigates reactive behavior toward them.

We can discern whether it is better to speak up or remain silent. We have no desire for separation in our righteousness. We would rather remain in balance with Unconditional Love than to be right and in separation. When a situation needs more understanding before resolution, we can offer compassion instead of judgment. We feel empowered operating in the Mode of Love. In our joy and in our pain, we receive, feel, and give Unconditional Love in a conscious relationship with the Source of Unconditional Love. We appreciate the impact of our Personal Heart Power!

The Whole Personal Heart State

Finally, in this state:

- The Personal Heart is in total alignment with an open Personal Heart and calm mind in union with the Source of Unconditional Love. Separation from the Source of Unconditional Love does not exist.
- There is no range of experience. It is an experience of enlightenment. It is the experience of wholeness and oneness where the illusion of separation no longer exists.
- Thoughts are no longer personalized and are flowing into us as wisdom, instruction, or knowing from the Source of Unconditional Love. Stress Loops have dissipated as our thoughts are now one with Unconditional Love.
- Feelings are high vibrational, clear, and accurate as they guide us to remain in this Whole Personal Heart State. We can emotionally process through what life brings us.
- We perceive choices in the present moment guided by Unconditional Love versus discernment. We make choices for the good of the whole.
- Behaviors solely operate from Unconditional Love. Our behavior is beneficial for us *and* others. We offer love and gratitude in return for *all* experiences we have.

In the Whole Personal Heart State, the beach home is our dream home. It is immaculate and sacred. The four pillars can weather any storm and will support the home eternally. The rooms seem magically pristine with everything we would dream of. When we switch on the lights, we only see beauty. Everything works as if it were brand new. Looking at the home fills our heart with joy and peace. This is the home we are meant to have. We offer gratitude for being blessed for this moment and for this home—our new sanctuary.

Like the beach home, our Personal Heart in the Whole State is heaven on earth. It is blissful and serene in union with the Source of Unconditional Love. We function optimally and feel the abundance of Unconditional Love. The connection between the Personal Heart and calm mind has developed into a complete and loving union. There are no words to describe the magnificent magnitude of this union.

This state holds miracles, synchronistic moments, and spontaneous healings. There is no separation from Unconditional Love as we become one with the Source of Unconditional Love. Even fear has been integrated with Unconditional Love because there is nothing—*nothing*—separate from Unconditional Love in this Personal Heart State. Separation is an illusion. It turns out the mystics know what they are talking about. We have mastered the beauty of Personal Heart Power. We may create the world we desire with ease and grace. Intention and manifestation have replaced the effort we put into trying. Most people find holding this Personal Heart State extremely challenging. This is what we can aspire to and journey toward.

All aspects of the Personal Heart and mind are operating with Unconditional Love. If a Personal Heart Pillar or Chamber goes out of balance, we shift to another Personal Heart State. This makes this Personal Heart State precarious to achieve and maintain.

In this state, we have made conscious decisions in our thoughts, feelings, and behaviors to operate from the Mode of Love to the point where we operate in this Mode continuously. We create and experience our desires and intentions with conscious awareness connecting and operating with Unconditional Love.

With a more expanded perspective and understanding of the Personal Heart States, we have the information of how each state perceives the reality of life. In the five Personal Heart States, the same experience can be perceived differently, which explains why different people perceive the same situation with varied conclusions about what occurred.

With our Personal Heart Power, we can consciously know our Personal Heart State and what we need to maintain or shift to the Personal Heart State we desire. The relevance of the Personal Heart States in relationship to the other aspects of the Personal Heart—Chambers, Pillars, Functions, and Modes of Operation—creates the foundation of what we need to recognize and connect to our Personal Heart Power.

Now that you have the foundational framework of your Personal Heart structure, it's time to explore the sequencing section. This is where we'll explore moving from self-love, to choice, to transition, and transformation. Utilizing this sequence in conjunction with the Personal Heart Power framework ultimately leads to your Personal Heart Power.

Fear to

Love

Introduction

We are on this path to a more love-focused life with this Personal Heart Power framework. It is powerful when we make the transformation from the Mode of Fear to the Mode of Love, with fear as our informant. Understanding and using the Personal Heart Chambers, Pillars, Functions, and States from the Mode of Love, on a conscious level, helps us make choices that shift us towards a greater capacity to love.

Applying what we have learned, and gaining awareness in our Personal Heart, frees us to shift from the Mode of Fear to the Mode of Love. The process of shifting our Personal Heart begins by recognizing what we love about ourselves and what we would like to change. We call this a *Transition Point.

A Transition Point is the moment we allow a transitioning process to begin towards a new way of being. This may happen consciously or subconsciously. Ideally, we want to transition consciously so that we operate from our Personal Heart Power. Transition takes time, practice, intention, and patience. The transitioning process is not an overnight success or a quick fix. Think of it as more of a lifestyle change. Or better yet, make this a lifestyle practice.

In this section, we will use the information learned from the previous section and understand how it influences our ability to love ourselves. Self-love is the key to our dream home, the key to shifting from the Mode of Fear to the Mode of Love. We now have enough information and awareness to *lead* our life instead of life leading *us*!

This can be an exciting phase! This does not mean we will no longer have challenges in our life or that we can always function in optimal balance. Instead, it means that we will have a different relationship with these challenges. This loving relationship allows us to experience more calmness, clarity, openness, and confidence from a perspective of Unconditional Love.

This Unconditional Love-focused perspective is living consciously in our open Personal Heart with a calm mind. A love-focused life can turn into reality through our belief in choice. Transition Points emerge when we have a greater ability to trust ourselves in the decision-making process.

When we say, "Yes," to our Personal Heart Power journey at a Transition Point, a *Transformational Sequence begins. **A Transformational Sequence is a series of choices rooted in love that lead to greater Personal Heart Power.** A Transformational Sequence begins with loving ourselves and being able to take in love from others. This self-love allows us to make more loving choices, helping us to begin our transition into a more love-focused life. Practice, repetition, and consistency of loving choices will create a transformation into Personal Heart Power.

With this exciting news, let's dive deeper into the sequence that occurs to reach transformation in your Personal Heart.

CHAPTER 9

Self-Love

Imagine being in your dream home feeling safe, appreciating all you have done to make it your dream home, and the complete sense of joy and love you feel in the moment. You are feeling content with who you are. It is easy for anyone to recognize this dream home has been cared for and loved. It's not the size and the value, it's the love and the care of the home that matters. Just like the imagined dream home, it is the love and care you put into yourself that matters.

Self-love is the ability to love yourself unconditionally. Dictionary.com definition says self-love means the "Regard for one's own well-being and happiness, chiefly considered as a desirable rather than a narcissistic characteristic." In contrast, when the terminology *self-love* first emerged in the sixteenth century, it was considered, unfavorably, as a form of narcissism. This shift of self-love over time reflects the evolution of humanity's perception of loving oneself. There is healthy self-love and narcissistic self-love, which might explain why it is difficult for some to accept loving themselves for fear of being perceived as narcissistic. We believe in healthy self-love and that will be our focus.

Many people are not consciously aware there is self-love, let alone a connection with their Personal Heart. The awareness that there is a Personal Heart rooted in self-love creates a new evolutionary paradigm. Advocates of self-love include Louise Hay, Brené Brown, Marianne Williamson, Carolyn Myss, Oprah Winfrey, Wayne Dyer, Gregg Braden, Deepak Chopra, the Dalai Lama, Anita Moorjani, Barbara Marx Hubbard, The HeartMath Institute, and the Good of the Whole, to name a few.

Within today's society, when we consciously talk about love, it is often from a romantic perspective. Our society typically views love as the deep, passionate love between life partners, the love between family members, or the conditional love of an unhealthy relationship. Often, these primary relationships are where we have our first awareness of love. Self-love is a relatively new paradigm in our culture. It continues to expand as a loving evolution.

We now recognize not only the importance of loving others but also the importance of loving ourselves. This dual intention presents a conundrum: which comes first, self-love or loving others? It's a bit like the classic conundrum: *Which came first: the chicken or the egg?* Part of the journey to our Personal Heart Power is exploring these questions and others, including:

- Do we need to love ourselves before we can love others, or do others need to love us before we can love ourselves?
- Is it possible to love others before we love ourselves?
- Can we normalize self-love as a daily practice without being narcissistic?
- Why is it important to normalize self-love as a practice?

The way to explore these questions is with awareness. It's beneficial to recognize what our capacity to love ourselves is now. This enables us to decide whether we are content with how we are loving ourselves or if we want to make some changes.

Often, we believe the ability to love ourselves depends upon the love received from others. Being aware of critical judgments from others can trigger critical judgment within ourselves. Self-judgment and believing others' judgments about us can close our Personal Heart to love. Self-love is the ability to love and accept ourselves unconditionally, no matter what someone else says or believes about us. Keep in mind this does not mean that we disregard everything people say. They may offer information that could be beneficial for our growth.

Before self-love became accepted as healthy, society commonly believed that love came from external sources. We would search for love from other people or something outside of us. Many songs express the successes and failures of looking outside oneself for love. Personal Heart Power grows when we expand the understanding that love comes from both external and internal resources.

Unconditional self-love is the most powerful love to operate within our Personal Heart and to connect to our Personal Heart Power. Looking back to the chicken or egg conundrum, our *egg* may be someone else's *chicken*. Getting stuck in the question of, *Do I need self-love first or love from others first?* distracts us from our journey to connect to our Personal Heart Power. For some, practicing self-love regularly will help in the efforts to maintain operating from the Mode of Love. For others, taking in external love activates the efforts into developing self-love by facilitating a shift into the Mode of Love. In this mode, loving ourselves unconditionally becomes reality, and self-love makes the transformation to Personal Heart Power possible.

With self-love, we find the courage to use clarity and confidence to do what is necessary to stay in or move back into balance, even when it is challenging in the present moment. Self-love gives us the courage to observe our feelings and explore our Personal Heart with more conscious awareness, kindness, and compassion. As our self-love expands, our dependence upon others' validation of us diminishes. This self-love depends upon the internal relationship we have with ourselves.

We live on a dynamic continuum that can range from self-hatred to unconditional self-love. To assess our self-love in this moment, on a scale of one to ten, where one is no self-love and ten is unconditional self-love, rate how much you believe the statement: *I am lovable.* Any number below ten gives insight into the limitations you might be placing on yourself for being worthy of self-love. The more you explore the limitations that keep you from loving yourself unconditionally, the more likely you will make choices to transform your limitations into opportunities for more self-love.

The awareness that there is Personal Heart Power is a new evolutionary paradigm that supports loving yourself. Being open to a new belief system around self-love makes it possible to recognize the importance of the Mode of Operation regarding self-love.

It is difficult to feel a conscious awareness of self-love when we operate from the Mode of Fear. Lower vibrational energy restricts us to self-judgment, self-resentment, self-denial, non-acceptance, and, at best, conditional self-love. It is here that we stay stuck living with a stressful mind functioning in lower vibrational Stress Loops that don't allow the Personal Heart to operate effectively.

We become dependent on love as an informant from external sources to spark that light within us. Remember, it is the Mode of Love operating in higher vibrational energy that allows us to connect with self-love in our Personal Heart. A higher vibrational energy allows us to open ourselves for opportunities of self-compassion, self-forgiveness, self-acceptance, and unconditional self-love. It also enables us to offer these practices to others.

There are many layers of conditions between self-hatred and self-love. Each conditional layer is a representation of how we close love off to ourselves. Some descriptors of conditional layers include self-judgment, judgment from others, personal stressful beliefs, others' stressful beliefs, negative self-talk, lower vibrational behaviors, and feelings fueled by fear. When we are ready to eliminate some of these layers, opportunities to release them can appear. With self-love, we can recognize these opportunities to let go of these layers in ways we could not before. Reading this book and using the tools is an example of one such opportunity.

Self-love is the key to opening our Personal Heart to the Source of Unconditional Love. It is one way we can transition from the Mode of Fear to the Mode of Love. To shift to the Mode of Love, we need to think or feel a hint of love. If we are at the extreme of self-hatred, the information and love needed to shift our perception initially comes from external sources.

When we have an inkling to buy a book, see a movie, meet a new friend, get a new job, sign up for a workshop or class, go to an AA meeting, or any other similar synchronistic opportunity, consider it as an external prompt trying to support an internal desire. It could also be an internal desire seeking external support. The teacher will show up in some form when we are ready to move forward on our journey.

Once we can sustain self-love, we are more able to remain operating in the Mode of Love. When we practice self-love more consistently, our desire to maintain it becomes more desirable. With more self-love, we are more likely to be aware of when we shift into the Mode of Fear. This awareness allows us to make conscious choices to shift back to the Mode of Love. When we operate from the Mode of Love, we perceive and sense the energy flowing in and out of our Personal Heart and how it affects our ability to love ourselves and others.

Our Personal Heart Power is when we do not feel the need to change ourselves to receive the love of others. Rather, we seek others who will love and support us in our love-focused journey.

This is functioning with a healthy self-love. This allows a healthier relationship to form with ourselves and others.

*Conditional love is love with prerequisites or expectations. This type of love relies on other people to love us the way we want to be loved or to change ourselves so they will love us. It is a love rooted in fear.

Again, the concept of self-love is the ability to love ourselves unconditionally in a healthy, non-narcissistic way. What does the term *unconditionally* really mean in relation to self-love? It means there are no blockages to the flow of love. No matter what we think, feel, or do, we love ourselves. With self-love, we may have thoughts, feelings, or behaviors we would like to change, but we will feel love for ourselves anyway as we journey to change them. Self-love creates a healthy Personal Heart connection rooted in love.

Self-love operates from the Mode of Love. When we operate from love, we have access to a cornucopia of tools, including forgiveness, acceptance, empathy, and compassion. These tools allow us to resolve challenges within ourselves and with others in a healthy way. We also develop greater awareness and appreciation of which practices work to keep us in the Mode of Love.

We can appreciate all our flaws, strengths, weaknesses, and abundances of life, and use them for empowerment and growth. Loving ourselves allows us the ability to be more present and conscious to make the healthy decisions we need for our journey.

Self-love empowers us to lead our life rather than letting life lead us. Fear becomes our informant and not our crippling ruler. We feel good and hopeful as we recognize the possibility of each situation moving us towards greater love. Self-love keeps us in the higher vibrational field of thoughts, feelings, and behaviors. We live and focus from an open Personal Heart, which allows us to see the world for the beautiful place it is. Self-love also allows you to recognize and enjoy the wonderful, beautiful, amazing you! It is the internal golden love thread that does not get severed during life's challenges.

This golden thread depends on the balance of the various aspects of the Personal Heart. The more self-love we embody, the more likely we are to make choices rooted in the Mode of Love in our Personal Heart. By loving ourselves, we have the ability to shift our Personal Heart State, Chambers, Pillars, and Functions when they are out of balance. This allows for operating optimally in our Personal Heart. This is the reward of self-love through self-care, which keeps us in the present moment and operating from the Mode of Love. This creates more balance for a love-focused life.

With daily self-love practices, we can move more swiftly from lower vibrational energy to higher vibrational energy throughout our day. Being able to move more swiftly to this higher vibrational energy has the most loving effect on our life—making our choices from the Mode of Love.

CHAPTER 10

Choice

Think about the number of choices you make every moment of every day. Consider the choices you make consciously. Now try to imagine all those unconscious decisions you make: walking, drinking, laughing... isn't it amazing how many choices we make as we journey through our day?

Choice can either enhance the reality we want to create in our life or it can cripple it. Believing in choice can empower our Personal Heart Power! When we are consciously aware that the choices we make create our reality, we begin to make choices that create the life we want to live. The Mode of Fear and Love energizes our choices.

The thread through this book has been how our Mode of Operation influences our outcomes in life. How it influences our choices is no exception. Most often, choices are an unconscious, ongoing process, which means that many of them are habitual. We may not even be aware we're making those choices, because the belief of choice is based on our level of consciousness in our Personal Heart and mind and our Mode of Operation.

If we function at an unconscious level in the Mode of Fear, our choices seem very limited. If we function at a high level of consciousness from the Mode of Love, we will see a wide range of options. Once we recognize there are choices, we are at a *Choice Point. A **Choice Point is the moment when we are consciously aware we have a choice and then we make a conscious decision rather than a subconscious one.**

A common Choice Point follows the completion of school. Just stop and think for a moment about this Choice Point in your life. How did you choose the path you followed next? Did you consciously review all the choices available to you? How many choices did you see at that time? Was this time of choosing filled with the perception of abundant opportunity or many limitations?

In 1983, the year I (Michelle) graduated from high school, 73.5% of females and 74.4% of males graduated from high school.[14] Four years later, which is the typical time to earn a college degree, only 16.5% of females graduated with a four-year degree and 23.6% of males.[15]

I did not know these statistics when I graduated from high school. In my mind, everyone graduated from high school and almost everyone in my class was going to college. I have no idea why I drew that conclusion. I know I put little conscious thought into the opportunities before me. I just knew I wanted to go to college, even though I did not completely understand what that meant.

Looking back, it feels like going to college was an impulse instead of a conscious decision-making process. I cannot find the Choice Point, but I do see the series of choices I made that followed the impulse. Nowhere along the way did I stop and consciously weigh the pros and cons of my choices. I made them based on very little information or thought.

My parents suggested I speak to the school counselor because they did not know how to guide me in this college choice; I was the first in our family to go. Although I had never gone to the school counselor before, he became an obvious choice for my next step in life.

I remember being both excited and nervous about the conversation. It was as if I could feel the transition that would follow my choices to get to college, but I was not consciously feeling or thinking anything.

I remember it as if it were yesterday, mustering up my courage and sharing, with the youthful vigor of possibility, my college dream with the school counselor. He listened, which further fueled my courage. I paused and was ready for the wisdom I needed to make my dream a reality.

"Why would you go to college when you could go to the cosmetology school here and take over your dad's business?" he said.

My head spun. I tried to find clarity in an answer I had not expected. Internally, I screamed, "What did he just say?"

My mind decided I must have misunderstood him. It must have been one of those sarcastic jokes people sometimes say that usually confuses me. I chose to come back with a bit of humor. "Because my dad told me I could come back home, but first I needed to get the hell out of town and see some of the world."

There was no laughter because there was no joke.

"What do you want me to do about that?" he asked.

I remember feeling confused. I did not know what to do. "Can you give me some school applications?" That seemed a sensible question. He was the school counselor, after all.

Shockingly, he shook his head. "I can't help you with that."

I was overwhelmed and did not know what to do. I sat stunned and silent.

"Is there anything else I can help you with?" he asked.

Unable to think of anything, I got up and left.

As I stepped out of his office, I felt all of my feelings rise to the surface: abandonment, loneliness, sadness, fear, and disappointment. I lost hope of going to college. Tearful, and alone in the empty school hallway, I felt completely deflated. I couldn't see any choices in front of me. It really can happen that quickly when we operate subconsciously and put the power of opportunity totally in the hands of someone else.

At that moment, and for as long as I can remember, when faced with similar difficulties—often unconsciously—I whispered and prayed, "God, what am I supposed to do now?"

Just as I finished the question, one of my best friends came around the corner with a hall pass for a bathroom break. She was about to say, "Hello," when she saw me crying.

"What's wrong?" she asked.

I shared my heartbreaking story with my sense of defeat.

Casually, but confidently, she said, "My dad is helping me with my college applications and I'm sure he would help you too."

Suddenly, I felt like I could go to college, after all!

Neither my friend nor her dad remembers helping me fill out college applications, but I do. I felt like I'd won the lottery that day. I know it wrote on my soul, so I would remember there are always more choices than the ones right in front of me. If I want to function from my Personal Heart Power, it is my responsibility to remain open for choices to show up, to seek ones when they don't, and to explore consciously all choices available to me.

When we intentionally choose to live within our Personal Heart with consciousness, we can recognize how choices are different between the Mode of Fear and the Mode of Love.

At the beginning of our lives, someone else primarily makes our choices for us. We were born into a specific modeling from our primary caregivers and the choices they made. Their fluctuations between fear and love within their Personal Hearts influenced the Mode of Operation in our Personal Heart. We probably unconsciously imprinted and integrated these ways of operation and perceived them as normal ways of being. If one Mode—Fear or Love—operates dominantly in our family, that Mode becomes particularly influential in our Personal

Heart. The behaviors of those around us influence the choices we make. This influence can be conscious or unconscious in our decision-making process. Personal Heart Power comes when we can choose consciously if we desire to allow that influence to affect our life or not.

Think back to your childhood. Consider how each of your parents or primary caregivers modeled fear and love in your home. Notice how their Mode of Operation affected your Personal Heart while growing up. These childhood experiences with your caregivers have directly influenced your relationship with fear and love. Just pause for a moment to think about this. Notice the feelings—without judgment. What do you experience in this moment as you remember your past? It's valuable to write down these feelings and any other triggered thoughts and memories. Celebrate the joyful ones and remember, you can process through the painful ones when you can consciously remember them!

If we apply this information through a common everyday scenario of childhood, such as the seemingly simple task of having breakfast, we can see how the Personal Heart State of a caregiver affects the reality of the situation. Each of the following scenarios presents a different outcome depending upon the different Personal Heart States. Try to imagine these scenarios with a calm mind and an open Personal Heart to give you a more accurate perception of them, without judgment. We recognize some of you may have had a different primary caregiver, but for clarity and consistency of reading, we chose the primary caretaker in our scenarios to be a mom.

As you read through the various scenarios, be aware that they may trigger memories and feelings for you. Some of these may be uncomfortable. Take the time to care for yourself if lower vibrational feelings are triggered. You might also want to record in a journal what you experience as you read the different scenarios. Keep in mind that this is about how the caretaker's Personal Heart State can greatly influence the functioning of a child.

Scenario 1

In this example, your mom is operating from the Disconnected Personal Heart State. You are getting ready for school and are in a good mood. You come down for breakfast, being mindful to listen for your mom's footsteps. You have no desire to find out what kind of mood she is in today. Typically, it's not a good one. You feel relieved to have the kitchen to yourself. Relief quickly shifts when you hear your mom's footsteps approaching. This is your cue to leave. Your fight, flight, or freeze reaction immediately engages. You do not want her to see you for fear she will darken your mood. You choose the flight reaction and quickly grab your toast and run out the door.

Your experiences with your mom in the Disconnected Personal Heart State have taught you that interactions with her often end in an undesirable conflict. The regular experience of conflicts with her can create a disconnection between both Personal Hearts. In this type of relationship, there is a tendency for avoidance.

Scenario 2

In this example, your mom is operating from the Reactive Personal Heart State. You are getting ready for school and have come down for breakfast. Today you have the kitchen to yourself, and you feel relief as you place a piece of bread in the toaster. The relief quickly shifts when you hear your mom's footsteps.

She comes into the kitchen. "You are making me a piece of toast too, right?"

You tense up to her questioning and immediately add another slice of bread to the toaster. "Yes, there is a piece of toast for you, too."

She stares at you. "You hoped I wouldn't catch you putting in that piece of toast. You had no intention of making me breakfast, did you?"

You stay silent, hoping you will not spark another judgmental reaction from her. You knew you needed to make your mom happy in this moment to avoid more judgments or conflict with her. The easiest way to avoid more of her reactionary behaviors is to please her. This is how it feels to live in fear.

In this scenario, your mom is operating from the Mode of Fear. As a child, you are on an emotional roller coaster ride with your mom. It is typical in situations like this for the child to react with a fight, flight, or freeze response.

Scenario 3

In this example, your mom is operating from the Half-hearted Personal Heart State. You are getting ready for school and are coming down for breakfast. Today you have the kitchen to yourself. Soon you hear your mom's footsteps.

She breaks the silence. "Good morning."

"Good morning," you reply. She seems to be in a pretty good mood today. Better than she has been on other days. "I'm making some toast. Would you like some?" you enquire, as you place some bread in the toaster.

"That's OK. I am not ready to eat yet."

This seems like a good morning to ask her for the favor of driving you to your friend's house after school.

When your mom is in the Half-hearted State, you recognize the signs of when your mom is operating from the Mode of Fear or Love. Often as a child, you do this subconsciously based on the outcomes of previous experiences with her in each Mode of Operation. Sometimes the loving connection is felt and sometimes it is not.

Scenario 4

In this example, your mom is operating from the Content Personal Heart State. You are getting ready for school and are coming down for breakfast. As you come downstairs, you smell the toast your mom is making.

"Good morning," she says, as you enter the kitchen.

"Morning. May I have my favorite, peanut butter and honey, on my toast, please?" you ask.

"Of course you may." Lovingly, she puts in some bread for you. "So, what are you up to today?"

"I'm going to the football game tonight. I'm going with my friends and really looking forward to it."

"That's right," she nods. "You did mention that. Have fun with your friends. I hope the team wins."

When your mom is in the Content Personal Heart State, you feel her loving connection through her actions, like making breakfast and asking about your day. You want to share it with her.

Scenario 5

In this example, your mom is operating from the Whole Personal Heart State. You are getting ready for school and are coming down for breakfast. As you come downstairs, you smell the toast your mom is making.

"Good morning," she says, as you enter the kitchen.

"Good morning, Mom!" You inhale deeply. "I love the morning smell of breakfast!"

She smiles. "What would you like on your toast this morning?"

"My favorite: peanut butter and honey."

"Coming right up. So, what are you up to today?"

"I have a test in math today."

"Oh. How do you feel about that?"

"Nervous. It has been a challenging unit for me."

She smiles at you. "You have been challenged before in math and somehow you figured out a way through it. Is there anything I can help you with this morning?"

"No, I don't think so. But thanks for offering."

You both sit down and enjoy your toast together before you head off to school. You feel loved, heard, cared for, and ready to face the challenge of your day: the math test.

This loving relationship is supported not only by the caring actions of the mom but also by her ability to empathize with and honor your feelings.

In these five scenarios, the different realities change depending upon your mom's Personal Heart State and whether she operated from the Mode of Fear or the Mode of Love. This, in turn, affected your Mode of Operation. Did you feel the different lower and higher vibrational energies in each scenario? Did you recognize the different outcomes based on these energies? This is how the Personal Heart manages the energies that ebb and flow throughout our day. Our perceptions of the energies then determine the choices we have based on whether we are operating from the Mode of Fear or Love.

Modes of Operation are often acquired through the conditioning actions of our caregivers unless we make choices to shift our Mode of Operation. Our caregivers are not solely responsible for us as we grow up. As we experience more in life, we make our own choices of what we believe and how we operate from our Personal Heart. We also see the different ways people operate in these modes of Fear and Love. These different ways also influence our way of operating in our Personal Heart.

Over time, we find it easier to determine at a Choice Point whether a choice will enhance, maintain, or take us away from balance in our Personal Heart. Choice is determined by our perspective, which is driven by our Mode of Operation. Our perspective is the story we carry in our Personal Heart and mind. Perspective is how we perceive our life in direct relation to how we choose to live our life. This becomes our story.

With each choice, we determine if we will continue to validate our current story or change to a new one. We control what our story is by choice or by default. The Modes of Fear or Love become the filters that determine our perspective on our choices. And it's our perspective of our story that directly influences our thoughts, feelings, and behaviors regarding the choices we make and the balance within our Personal Heart.

With awareness, we can recognize how our choices shift and change the outcomes in our life. This conscious awareness of choice presents the opportunity for us to do something different or not. This awareness also gives us the ability to recognize our choices and choose the higher vibrational ones. Understanding the significance of our choices, whether lower or higher vibrational, will influence our Personal Heart Power.

Moving our experiences from the autopilot of making habitual lower vibrational choices into the consciousness of higher vibrational choices will create the love-focused life we desire. We will then make choices aligned with our desired way of being in the world. In conscious awareness, we may need to feel some essential pains and discomforts in the decision-making process, but we can process through these pains more effectively with emotional processing practices.

We can effectively process the essential pains by intentionally learning and practicing tools and skill sets. We'll cover tools that can process through the lower vibrational feelings and discern optimal choices in Section 3. The choice to process the lower vibrational feelings allows for a more informed and conscious decision-making process.

There are three different effects choices can have on our life. They will either:

- move us forward,
- keep us where we are,
- or hold us back from where we want to go.

Being conscious of these choices allows us to determine intentionally which effect we prefer from the choices available to us.

When we have the courage to feel the discomfort or joy life gives us, we are more likely to recognize more choices. This discernment allows us to determine what we need in the moment to recognize what choices will benefit us. The recognition of choices moves us into that deeper connection to self—a deeper understanding of our Personal Heart. This, in turn, gives us a deeper comprehension of our thoughts, feelings, and the choices we make, which become our behaviors.

Choices made consciously empower us to make more of them so we can operate from the Mode of Love. In the moment of awareness, we can decide consciously if we want to operate from the Mode of Fear or Love regarding whatever life presents to us.

When our Mode of Operation is primarily Fear, it limits our perception or ability to recognize the range of choices available to us. Rather than the optimal long-term solution, Fear wants the quickest resolution to a problem to eliminate or reduce pain quickly.

The Mode of Fear is in survival mode to get through the moment with minimal regard for the future. Fear wants to be in control because control creates the perception of safety. Fear chooses a fight, flight, or freeze response to feelings. Choices fueled by the Mode of Fear may restrict and close the Personal Heart.

As a result, in fear, we only consider choices offering quick results with the perception of less pain and more safety. However, short-term choices can lead to long-term pain, but the Mode of Fear does not recognize other available choices. In our society, we have created a stressful belief that if we make a *perfect choice*, we will not need to feel any pain or cause any pain to others. This stressful belief is a misconception. Essential pain can be a part of the decision-making process even when it is our optimal choice, so it is an illusion to think we can make a *perfect choice* to avoid all pain.

Unconscious coping behaviors activate to resist, avoid, or numb the stressful feelings. Some coping behaviors include over or under eating, too much television or technology, excessive drinking, smoking, overworking, overspending, people-pleasing, excessive or lack of exercising, or misusing drugs. These behaviors ultimately take us out of balance. In some cases, when an unfamiliar higher vibrational choice is presented to us, it may make us feel vulnerable. In this situation, we may sabotage the higher vibrational choice by making a habitual, lower vibrational choice.

When making choices, it is common to think in terms of *right* or *wrong* choices. The fear of making the wrong choice can keep us stuck in indecision. The stress of being wrong can be so overwhelming it prohibits decision-making. This indicates we are in the Mode of Fear.

In the Mode of Fear, love is the informant and becomes the driver to make different, higher vibrational choices. When we have consciousness, we gain more awareness of our feelings. When there has been enough pain, we find the courage to make a different choice. Personal Heart Power comes when we have the awareness that we can choose from the Mode of Love versus the Mode of Fear. In the Mode of Love, we can begin to shift our decision-making from wondering if our choice is *right* or *wrong* to how is this a *loving* choice? This awareness moves us from default choices to more conscious ones.

When we operate from the Mode of Love, we choose to process through our feelings to determine what optimal behaviors can move us back to balance or how to stay in balance. Choices fueled by the Mode of Love may open the Personal Heart and expand our perceptions of choice.

We recognize the array of choices and their potential long-term effects on our life. With each choice, we consider how it is loving for our life. We know we can determine our needs and make choices to meet those needs.

To take care of our needs, we first must discover what they are. One way is to ask ourselves, "How do I feel?" and "What do I need?" These basic questions present relevant information to determine what we need to do to get into balance or stay in balance. Our Mode of Operation influences our answers to these two questions. Typically, in the Mode of Love, our choices focus on balance.

Choices are pivotal in life. The consequences of our choices determine the reality we experience. These consequences may be on a continuum, from being detrimental to being beneficial for us. Operating from the Mode of Fear or the Mode of Love shifts our perception of what choices we have in the moment. Conscious choice empowers the reality we want to create in our life. When we have reached the conscious awareness that our belief in choices creates our reality, it becomes possible to live the life we *choose* to lead. A series of consistent choices rooted in Love ultimately brings us to the point of transition from the Mode of Fear to the Mode of Love. It takes practice to operate more often from the Mode of Love. In relation to Personal Heart Power, it is necessary to take responsibility for our choices to tap into our power. This means recognizing choices and making a *loving* choice that supports a love-focused life.

CHAPTER 11

Transition

Our Personal Heart journey starts with awareness, then moves to higher vibrational choices, which creates the transition to a more love-focused life. When we transition to our Personal Heart Power, our heart becomes more open and aligned with the Source of Unconditional Love. The first transitions typically start with the desire to move into higher vibrational choices so we can feel better in our life. **Transition is a series of consistent choices rooted in higher vibrational thoughts, feelings, and behaviors.**

The transition to Personal Heart Power is when, at the Transition Point, we begin to choose a series of love-focused decisions to move towards a more loving way of being in our Personal Heart.

The Personal Heart Power journey entails transitioning to a more open Personal Heart, and this depends on our daily choices. Our choices determine our relationship with ourselves, others, our environment, and the Source of Unconditional Love. Healthy daily choices support us in remaining in or restoring balance to our Personal Heart. For example, when faced with the opportunity of a new job, marriage, moving, or more education, what are the choices we can make from our open Personal Heart and calm mind to transition to a more love-focused life?

Not every decision plays a primary role in a transitioning process—that would be daunting. However, some smaller decisions can play a role if we realize they are not beneficial for our transitioning process. For example, if we discover a company from which we buy our cleaning products financially supports an organization that goes against our core values, we can buy from another company that shares our values.

Awareness of our Personal Heart State helps us to make choices that can transition us into our next desired Personal Heart State. We know our Personal Heart Power is engaged when we are making choices to remain in or transition to higher vibrational Heart States.

Whichever Personal Heart State we are in, our perception of available choices will be determined by the thoughts, feelings, and behaviors of that state. Through our consciousness, we can make higher vibrational choices that will transition us to our desired Personal Heart State and a calmer mind. Without conscious awareness, the choices we make are usually out of habit. If we want different results, we cannot keep doing the same thing over and over. If we want different results, we need to make different choices! This is more likely to happen when we are aware of our transitioning in our decision-making process.

Transitioning to a more open Personal Heart can feel unfamiliar from our previous ways of being. Even when we desire the transition, this unfamiliarity has the potential to feel confusing, uncomfortable, and vulnerable. When we make conscious decisions, we're more likely to trust the transitioning process and find the courage, strength, trust, and tenacity to follow through, even in the discomfort. With more practice, we feel empowered to make more conscious choices. We follow through because we know when we get through this transitioning period, we will create the love-focused life we desire.

Let's go back to the story of my (Grace's) first day of life when I disappointed my family: I put my mom through a long and painful labor; I disappointed my father because I was not a boy; I was born on my aunt's wedding day; I came out with a crooked face. Well, finally, on my thirty-second birthday, I summoned enough courage to make the request to my grandmother that she stop telling me that story about my first day of life. I couldn't help being born on that day, as a girl, with a crooked face!

Only then did my grandmother explain that she was crying because I was her first grandchild—not because I had a crooked face. Imagine, in that moment, how both of our perceptions shifted around my birth story! She never shared that story again, and I began transitioning that perception of my birth story. My request transitioned our relationship to a more loving way of relating to each other because I felt seen, heard, and understood by her.

When we are looking at transition in relation to our Personal Heart, we will also need to consider the transitions from the Mode of Fear to the Mode of Love. There is no set amount of time for transitions from a fear-based to a more love-focused life. Determining the time needed for transitions is difficult because it depends upon many factors.

During our transitions, we may be tempted to judge ourselves in relation to time because we are not meeting an expectation we set or that we perceive others have set for us. Each transition to a more open Personal Heart takes its own time. The amount of time will depend upon past events in our lives, our desired future, the significance of the transition, and our ability to make choices during the transition most often from the Mode of Love. Our Personal Heart Power transition is a more expansive version of our open Personal Heart.

Transitions also involve getting our Personal Heart Chambers, Pillars, and Functions in optimal balance and functioning in the Mode of Love when we wish to transition to a more love-focused life.

With repetitive higher vibrational thoughts, feelings, and behaviors, it is possible to create more balance within all the aspects of the Personal Heart during transitional phases. One way of doing this is with a *reassuring statement. **A reassuring statement is a higher vibrational thought or statement used for transitioning into a calm mind.** Examples of reassuring statements include:

- *I am worthy.*
- *My feelings matter.*
- *I am good enough.*
- *I am safe.*
- *I am loveable.*

These higher vibrational thoughts will encourage higher vibrational feelings. These feelings typically lead to higher vibrational behaviors and a more balanced Personal Heart. Repeated higher vibrational choices will make it easier to transition to a more love-focused life. Each of the aspects of the Personal Heart plays a role in the many transitions shifting into the Mode of Love.

Transitions have no specific road map. Nor is there only one road to reach the destination of an open Personal Heart. There is an internal drive, but the directions are not necessarily clear. The transitions can be conscious or subconscious. They are not always smooth or straight; they can be chaotic, up and down, wavering, complicated, and downright frustrating at times, or the exact opposite. Sometimes, they can be direct and smooth, steady, simple, clear cut, and pleasant. These transitions are choices we can begin, abort, change, stifle, drag-out, delay, slow down, or complete. It is important to remember no one way works for everyone because this is *your* Personal Heart Power journey!

When we subconsciously transition, our perception is that the changes are happening *to* us, not *for* us. We have no awareness of choices or that transitions can be beneficial. We typically want to stay with what is predictable and what we know. For a loving transition to occur, the energetic driver is the Mode of Love.

With conscious awareness, we can recognize when a Choice Point could become a Transition Point. We are either making one choice at a Choice Point or we will choose to make a series of higher vibrational choices, which makes this a Transition Point. With awareness, we can recognize the opportunity for transition. We realize our current way of operating causes us enough discomfort that we want to consider different choices in our decision-making process. We might also realize our higher vibrational choices have had beneficial outcomes, which encourage us to continue making higher vibrational choices. These different choices are shifting us between our current way of being and a new way of being.

We may feel vulnerable at this point in transition because we have one foot in the old and one foot in the new. It creates an energetic teetering of perception as we consider which choice to make—to transition or not to transition—to what we desire. When we say "Yes," to transition at the Choice Point, we enter the Transition Point. We then create the change we desire by entering the transition process, consciously or unconsciously.

Typical life transitions include graduating from high school or college, getting our first job, finding a place to live, getting married, entering a committed relationship, or having a family. On a conscious level, these transitions become more intentional to transition us to a more love-focused life.

For example, perhaps your dream was to go to college to become a psychologist and ultimately have your own practice. In the beginning, you felt connected to this dream and connected to this profession. In your final year of college, you realize that much of what you have been taught does not resonate with your original dream. You now have to decide if you will continue as planned or choose to adjust your college experience, even if it may take more time.

The choices you make are creating the path you follow. At this Transition Point in your college experience, you may choose to continue a path that no longer fills your dreams, you may choose to transition to another major, or you may choose a totally different path by creating a new dream. These types of transitions occur often throughout life, whether or not you are consciously aware of them.

The Transition Points raise questions that lead to choices, consciously or subconsciously. We live with the lower and higher vibrational consequences of the choices we make, each one informing our journey differently. When we make decisions, we don't always have all the information about what the consequences of our choices might be. If we need to look back, avoid looking back in judgment or regret. Instead, look back with compassion and discernment so future choices can be well-informed. Let's explore transitioning through the Modes of Fear and Love.

In the Mode of Fear, fear is a crippler while love is trying to be the informant. In transitions, fear fuels the fight, flight, or freeze reaction that can override higher vibrational choices, which inhibits love-focused transitions. When fear is the crippler, it becomes challenging to transition to a more love-focused life.

We benefit most when we gain the conscious awareness that we need to get outside of the box of our current perceptions within the Mode of Fear to transition to the Mode of Love. Popular stories like Dr. Seuss's *How the Grinch Stole Christmas* and Charles Dickens's *A Christmas Carol*, are examples of how a character transitions from the Mode of Fear to the Mode of Love in their Personal Heart.

Support for transitioning can come from a movie or a book that opens our heart, from a gesture of kindness, Unconditional Love from another person or group, or from music or a song that touches our heart to feel that spark of Unconditional Love. These are Transition Points where we can make fear-based or love-focused choices. Transition Points lead to transition depending upon the vibrational quality of the choices we make. On the journey to our Personal Heart Power, we will need to make most choices from the Mode of Love.

During this transition period from Fear to Love, we might recognize Unconditional Love but are unable to use it effectively. As we continue to shift toward more conscious awareness and love-focused practices, our choices transition from a single decision being made from the Mode of Love to a series of love-focused decisions.

As we recognize the healthy feedback from our loving choices, we feel the higher vibrational feelings of love, joy, and peace. Simultaneously, we recognize the undesired feelings we receive from decisions based on fear. The love feelings create the desire to make more decisions from the Mode of Love. This is conscious awareness in transition. It is this awareness that allows us to make additional higher vibrational choices.

In the Mode of Love, fear becomes our informant, and Unconditional Love becomes our source of power. Unconditional Love becomes the crippler of fear and the primary energy in our love-focused life. When Unconditional Love is the primary energy during transition, we have a healthy relationship to fear. Typically, if we are operating in the Mode of Love, Unconditional Love allows us to operate from a calm mind and open Personal Heart more of the time.

As our Personal Heart Power expands, gratitude for fear as our informant and Love as our Mode of Operation becomes possible. Gratitude is an important part of this transitioning process, and it is one of the easiest ways to transition from Fear to Love. Appreciating our life makes it easier to transition into the Mode of Love because we know life is happening *for* us.

In the Mode of Love, fear continues to inform us of real dangers but does not cripple us with non-existent dangers. When we are balanced in our Personal Heart, we have an awareness of fear. We can recognize it is trying to guide us to make decisions that allow for the healthiest and safest outcomes given the situation. Fear informs us how to stay safe in challenging situations as we go through the transitioning process.

However, when fear gets out of balance, stressful moments become a temptation to make lower vibrational choices. This is when Stress Loops get triggered. When this happens, during the transitioning process, we become vulnerable to slipping back into the Mode of Fear. Some of these loops may trigger stressful beliefs which cause us to think we are unsafe, or we do not have enough of something, something is wrong, or that we are not good enough. When Stress Loops are activated, they can slow down, inhibit, and even reverse the transitioning process.

Patience through transition helps us to choose our next steps from this new way of being—operating in the Mode of Love with more conscious awareness, rather than our old way of being—in the Mode of Fear with less consciousness. Taking the time will help us mitigate the risk of moving too quickly and sliding back into lower vibrational thoughts, feelings, and behaviors.

With regular and consistent love-focused practices, we can reduce this oscillation between fear and love to transition into maintaining a love-focused life. As we stabilize our Personal Heart functioning based on the feedback from our higher vibrational and loving choices, we feel the higher vibrational feelings of love, joy, and peace. Simultaneously, we recognize the value of the lower vibrational feelings because they give us vital information about how we are going out of balance.

When we're operating in the Mode of Love, we understand it is important to process through these lower vibrational feelings, so we do not inhibit our transitioning and go into the Mode of Fear. We no longer need to go into the reactive decision-making process because we have transitioned to healthier practices to process through lower vibrational feelings. We can now come up with a choice that moves us towards a better balance, thus experiencing higher vibrational feelings. We are more aware of the value of transitioning into the Mode of Love with conscious awareness, and it's this awareness that allows us to make higher vibrational choices for optimal balance in all aspects of our Personal Heart.

At transition times, feelings often arise that evoke emotional responses. Keep in mind that any dramatic emotional response may cause an emotional overload in the Personal Heart. It is prudent in these moments to take incremental steps, so we feel safe to make our transitions.

The processing of feelings often accompanies transitions. We may choose to practice a tool, seek out loving support from other people, other resources, or perhaps we need a break. It is also empowering to have our experience witnessed, validated, and shared by another person or group with a loving presence. This is a way of honoring the transition to a more loving way of being.

The more we operate in the Mode of Love, with persistence and perseverance, using higher vibrational thoughts, feelings, and behaviors, the more this transition process becomes familiar. The more experiences we have in our new way of being, the less fear we feel in those experiences. The familiarity of transitioning in the Mode of Love becomes easier because feelings are more desirable in their higher vibrational frequency, even though the transitional process itself may be challenging.

Patience and pauses become a welcome part of the transitioning process as it moves us into a greater conscious awareness of living in the Mode of Love. The transitions bring more balance in our Personal Heart Chambers, Pillars, and Functions. We also gain a deeper awareness of being in the Mode of Love.

Transitioning into the Mode of Love leads to transformation. Transformation in our Personal Heart occurs when there is an acceptance of transition to operate continually in a loving way of being. Every time we say, "Yes!" to transition, in the Mode of Love, we are moving toward transformation in our Personal Heart for a more love-focused life. When we say, "Yes!" to transformation, we connect to more of our Personal Heart Power.

CHAPTER 12

Transformation

Not all transformations have the same effect on our life. They can make us feel more empowered or powerless. What may be empowering for us could be deflating for someone else. Some key moments in our life, such as when we get our college degree, get married, have children, move to another country, or say "Yes," to learning a new skill to enhance our life, would be considered transformations. They can be lower or higher vibrational, depending upon our perception of the situation.

Lower vibrational behaviors, like a path of addiction, doing something we know is not healthy for us, accepting a job promotion we don't want, or quitting something out of fear, are fueled by the Mode of Fear, which reduces our Personal Heart Power. Although each of these situations is a type of transformation, our intention here is to focus on the higher vibrational transformations that operate from the Mode of Love with our Personal Heart Power. Higher vibrational transformations will move us to more Personal Heart Power.

Dictionary.com defines transformation as "A thorough or dramatic change in form or appearance." Therefore, transformation in the

Personal Heart is a thorough or dramatic change in our Mode of Operation from Fear to Love. In our Personal Heart, **Transformation is a series of transitions that lead to the major shift from living life primarily from the Mode of Fear to living life primarily from the Mode of Love in our Personal Heart.** Transformation is a commitment to a new way of living our life and interacting with the world.

With conscious awareness, transformation can be a desired and intentional experience towards a more loving way of being. And when we're consciously aware of our choices as they arise, we can consciously choose how we want to use our Personal Heart Power. Barbara Marx Hubbard, an evolutionary visionary, stated it well: "You are the Life Force embodied at its next stage. When you are free of fear, the Life Force flows unimpeded and unconflicted as you."[16]

A common journey, and a simple way of looking at a transformation, are the *career* choices we make. Be it a job, profession, stay-at-home parent, artist, volunteer, or any of the multitude of options, we make many choices before we end up there. Each choice made is a potential transition toward our goal, consciously or unconsciously. When we get to our desired destination and we choose to integrate it as our love-focused life, we have made a transformation. If we choose not to integrate our choice, we will remain in transition.

This is a simplistic example of a foundational understanding of transformation within the Personal Heart. When we are looking at transformation in relation to our Personal Heart Power, our transformation occurs when we make empowering choices in transitioning from the Mode of Fear to the Mode of Love. It is about transitioning our Mode of Operation, Personal Heart Chambers, Pillars, and Functions to align and operate in the Personal Heart States fueled by the Mode of Love.

Let's imagine we are in the Half-hearted Personal Heart State, operating more often from fear than love. We are consciously aware of this, and we desire to take the steps to transition to a more loving way of being. One option to begin this process is by looking at the four Personal Heart Chambers. How does each one operate individually? As we look at the Energetic Chamber, we easily recognize our Half-hearted Personal Heart State. We know we can quickly shift from the higher vibrational energies to the lower vibrational energies with the littlest of annoyances. It benefits us that we recognize this easily. We can also choose to use the small annoyances to shift us to higher vibrational thoughts, feelings, and behaviors. Awareness guides us in the choices we need to make for our desired transformation.

As we move to the Physical Chamber, we recognize we take great care of ourselves. We eat well, have daily physical activity, and practice preventive health care. This Personal Heart Chamber appears balanced.

Looking at the Sensing Chamber, we realize we have been emotional lately and reactive in some situations—even overreactive—more frequently than desired. Transitioning to more emotional balance in this chamber would be beneficial.

Looking at our Spiritual Chamber, we experience a moment of clarity as we focus on our everyday reality. We realize we have a desire to be more love-focused but haven't started a regular practice yet.

Once we notice the chambers are out of balance, we can make choices to transition, bringing them back to balance. Maintaining this balance over time creates a transformation.

Can you see how the awareness of the balance in the chambers could support us in making more conscious choices for our love-focused life? First, we use this awareness to inform more loving choices for ourselves, then we move into transition. As we continue making these more loving choices through multiple transitions, operating from the Mode of Love, we gain more opportunities for those *Aha!* moments in our Personal Heart. Repetitive transitions ultimately become integrated as a new way of being in our life, which is a transformation.

We can continue this same type of practice to process through the Personal Heart Pillars and Personal Heart Functions. It is possible to transition in one or more of the Personal Heart Chambers, Pillars, or Functions at a time, as we experience the many moments of transitions in our journey. Chapter 14 provides an assessment tool to guide you in the evaluation of your Personal Heart.

Transitions are the shifting of energy from lower to higher vibrational frequencies. Thus, an energy transformation occurs as we transition into a more love-focused life. In his First Law of Thermodynamics, Albert Einstein emphasized that one cannot create or destroy energy; only transform it.[17] Ultimately, our willingness to go through each transition allows us to feel more self-love and connection to our Personal Heart. This type of conscious awareness eventually leads us to the transformation into our Personal Heart Power.

Moving into a loving transformation, we feel more Unconditional Love and compassion for ourselves and others. Our tendency for discernment increases as the need for judgment significantly lessens. We feel a greater sense of responsibility for our life. We find our courage with our Personal Heart Power. Our awareness rises, allowing us to recognize and appreciate the transitional journey we have completed to reach a transformation in our Mode of Operation. This allows a more loving way of being. Personal Heart transformation emboldens us to celebrate where we are and to continue consciously into the next phase of our love-focused journey.

How do we know we have made a series of transitions into a transformation of more Personal Heart Power? We operate differently, and we recognize that our life differs from what it was before. Having more Personal Heart Power means we feel a deeper connection to the Source of Unconditional Love. We know the difference between conditional love and Unconditional Love. We have a calmer mind, a keener sense of awareness, more compassion, more empathy, more peace, and we have transformed into a new and more loving way of being.

An important part of the transformation is accepting where we are in the moment. A transformation completes when we fully transition into a new way of being. We are more likely to avoid falling back to old, lower vibrational behaviors when we have reached transformation. In transformation, we have established daily loving practices into our routine. We stay transformed because operating from the Mode of Love feels more empowering.

In transition, we could go back to where we were, but we can't when we've reached transformation. This is because, even if we slip back into old habits, we now have more awareness of the consequences of the old, lower vibrational behaviors. In fact, it will probably take more numbing to remain in the closed Personal Heart as we surrender our Personal Heart Power to the Mode of Fear. Usually, our Personal Heart closes because we do not want to feel the pain, which can feel insurmountable at times.

Big triggers can activate setbacks. After a transformation, we are less likely to accept the setbacks because we have become more aware of the consequences of our lower vibrational thoughts, feelings, and behaviors. This greater awareness of challenging consequences typically motivates us to remain in or return to the new way of being.

In *The Evolutionary Testament of Co-Creation*, Barbara Marx Hubbard suggests, "Those of us who want to transform need only to set our focus on what we want to become, imagine ourselves as that desired being, and establish our heart with grace—that is, put loving trust in the mystery of nature: that it can create new forms out of old."[18] Knowing this may make it more bearable to experience essential pain during transition because we are aware that this pain will bring us to a more loving place. We keep making healthier choices because we know we feel better, which is desirable and ultimately can move us into transformation. Without that, we resist transformation.

The tipping point into transformation is when we know we have choices and we consciously make choices that move us to a more open

Personal Heart. This desired transformation happens because we want and are ready for the beauty of the transformation presenting itself to us. More Unconditional Love feels wonderful. When we are ready to feel it, we can believe we are worthy of it.

Transformation is about implementing love-focused options that we have discovered and practiced through the transitioning process. As we transform into our Personal Heart Power, we will recognize when we are shifting between the various Personal Heart States.

Can you sense how your awareness might allow connections to your Personal Heart? This awareness allows us to make healthier choices for ourselves to create the life we desire rooted in love. The choices we make from the Mode of Love increase the balance in our Personal Heart Chambers, strength in our Personal Heart Pillars, and more optimal functioning of our Personal Heart Functions.

If we are not willing to change our story, we cannot move into transformation! Transformation is the desire for change. If we would like a more love-focused life, we need a new story! We have the power to create one. It's our desire for a new Personal Heart story that brings us to our Personal Heart Power.

CHAPTER 13

Personal Heart Power

Our willingness to rewrite or add to our Personal Heart story continually allows us to reveal more of our Personal Heart Power. In an *Aha!* moment of transformation into the Mode of Love, we strengthen our ability to make choices to operate from our Personal Heart Power. This is the ability to choose higher vibrational thoughts, feelings, and behaviors intentionally, or to transform lower vibrational thoughts, feelings, and behaviors into higher vibrational ones.

Everyone experiences peaks and valleys in life, which challenges our ability to remain happy and in balance. Expecting to evolve into a life of pure happiness creates stress. However, we simply need to recognize that we have the power to restore balance from the challenges of life. That is the foundation of the Personal Heart Power journey. It's this awareness and desire to move into alignment between our Personal Heart and mind that makes it easier to use our Personal Heart Power.

Alignment is the connection or reconnection to our open Personal Heart and calm mind. This does not mean there is no chaos; it means we can remain calm *in* the chaos. Remember, we can stay calm in chaos when we are in balance or moving toward balance with the

Personal Heart Pillars, Chambers, and Functions and operating from the Mode of Love.

As we acknowledge the importance of balance in the various aspects of our Personal Heart, we recognize their interrelationship. Even when one aspect of our Personal Heart shifts to imbalance, the other aspects endure greater responsibilities as they attempt to compensate and hold our Personal Heart Power. Trying to manage this greater responsibility may then move other aspects into imbalance. When this happens, we can see how they may be overburdened and compromised to keep us from operating from our Personal Heart Power.

How do we know if we are connected to our Personal Heart Power? Let's go back to our dream home to answer this question.

In the comfort of our beach home, we feel content and connected to what we have created for our home. But one day, we notice the room darkening. From the window, we see the weather is changing. Across the ocean, dark clouds are rolling in, the waves are getting bigger, and the wind is picking up. This is not unfamiliar. At first, it seems manageable, but after a while, uncertainty grows within us. Before we know it, the waves are crashing at the pillars of our home, which is not typical in this weather.

If we are not connected with our Personal Heart Power, we are likely to spiral out into the Mode of Fear. This is when we feel the panic of the situation and our mind creates scenarios of destruction and chaos. We think about worst-case scenarios. In the storm's chaos, we cannot determine drama from reality.

We give fear the opportunity to take hold and fuel our behavior. It becomes nearly impossible to imagine survival. At this point, we have disconnected from our Personal Heart Power. Our Personal Heart and mind are unlikely to work together for the optimal outcome. Imagine how the various Personal Heart Chambers, Pillars, and Functions operate in this moment. Some of them are out of balance as we frantically feel the chaos of the situation.

When connected to our Personal Heart Power, we are in the calm of the storm. We are more likely to remain calm. We remember that this type of storm occurs several times a year, and our Personal Heart Pillars are built for them. We have built strong Personal Heart Pillars for a solid foundation of support. We have a plan prepared for safety should an unusual circumstance arise where we recognize risk. It does not mean fear is not present; it means fear is there as an informant to help guide our choices.

We know solutions for survival exist. We will make wise choices. This allows us to remain in balance and operate from the Mode of Love. This uses our Personal Heart Power. Imagine how the various Personal Heart Chambers, Pillars, and Functions operate in this scenario. Their ability to operate optimally allows us to remain calm in the storm.

With Personal Heart Power, the peaks and valleys in life remain. However, they become more manageable because we have developed practices to balance the Personal Heart Chambers, Pillars, and Functions in the Mode of Love, which allows a relationship with our Personal Heart Power. This is the relationship that empowers our life. To operate consistently from our Personal Heart Power requires ongoing practice, persistence, patience, and determination. Managing our Personal Heart Power is an ongoing, ever-changing journey throughout our life.

When present with our experiences, versus getting stuck in past or future stories, we notice the flow of information between the Personal Heart and the mind and whether we are operating from the Mode of Fear or the Mode of Love. Being present allows us the ability to process through the experiences of life with higher vibrational thoughts, feelings, and behaviors. Functioning from a higher vibrational Personal Heart State means the thoughts, feelings, and behaviors are rooted in the Mode of Love, which is our Personal Heart Power. How the Personal Heart Power establishes itself in an open Personal Heart connected to the calm mind is our superpower.

Our Personal Heart Power creates the ability for us to activate, shift, and stabilize from the Mode of Love within the Personal Heart Chambers, Pillars, and Functions, while intentionally doing the work to move into the Content or Whole Personal Heart State. This is unbelievably amazing, and no small feat to journey through and practice. We should recognize the magnitude of each step our journey takes that moves us towards a higher vibrational way of being. Celebrate the journey! To continually seek balance in the various aspects of our Personal Heart takes dedication to access our Personal Heart Power. Intentional changes take courage! Transformation pushes us to our edge to reach our desired outcome—our new love-focused life.

Thoughts continually run through our mind. Feelings flow from our Personal Heart. We engage in behaviors. Many thoughts, feelings, and behaviors are subconscious. It is unreasonable to be consciously aware of everything. Needing to be aware of every step, breath, movement, feeling, or action you experience is daunting and would be exhausting and impossible. However, with conscious or subconscious functioning, our Mode of Operation matters. It matters because the outcome is different based on the vibrational energy that is feeding our subconscious and conscious thoughts, feelings, and behaviors.

Our choices determine if we transition toward transformation to operate from our Personal Heart Power or not. Our Personal Heart Power lays dormant waiting for us to choose to activate it. It wants us to activate it. When we are ready, we will activate it.

Once we activate our Personal Heart Power and have achieved Personal Heart balance, we focus on how to manage our thoughts, feelings, and behaviors to keep us operating from the Mode of Love. The benefits of remaining in the Mode of Love include more clarity and recognition of a balanced Personal Heart. It feels wonderful!

Our perception of the world continues to expand and becomes more tolerant and inclusive of different perspectives. This gives us more freedom of choice, with which we can see the opportunity to choose more beneficial options for a love-filled life. We develop more acceptance, compassion, forgiveness, presence, balance, and, of course, love while we journey through life. It's our journey to discovering our Personal Heart Power that builds our dream home. It doesn't matter if this seems impossible or attainable. If we can imagine our Personal Heart Power, we can make it happen. So, make it happen!

Wherever you are on this journey to your Personal Heart Power, this is where you are meant to be today. And since you are reading this book, this means you are ready to activate it. Continue to take the courageous steps to operate from your Personal Heart Power.

The next step is to connect to, live from, and maintain your Personal Heart Power. In Section 3, we explore the variety of tools we practice to open our Personal Heart and calm our mind. These are the tools you can add to your Personal Heart Power toolbox.

Personal

Heart

Power

Toolbox

Introduction

Congratulations! You have now gained more insight, understanding, and awareness of your Personal Heart Power!

In this section, we present the tools to help you open your Personal Heart and calm your mind, which will enable you to ignite and ramp up your Personal Heart Power. There is no specific order of practice. Rather, the tools are a discovery of which ones are most effective for you in your current Personal Heart State. Some may seem quick and simple, yet very impactful in your process. That same tool can be extremely emotionally challenging when you are in another Personal Heart State. Therefore, an ongoing practice of exploration without judgment is the most beneficial as you determine what will work for you at this time. At another time, different tools may be more beneficial. Our hope is you will have fun in this exploration and enjoy the reward of practicing these tools for a more love-focused life.

Personal Heart Power Tools are specific practices for increasing your Personal Heart Power. These are tools that help bring ourselves into the present moment, increase conscious awareness, process thoughts and feelings, implement higher vibrational behaviors, calm the mind, open the Personal Heart, and connect with the Source of Unconditional Love.

These Power Tools can provide us with an increased capacity to love ourselves and others. Ideally, our toolbox will be filled with tools to help us make choices to build the life we desire—a life characterized by higher vibrational thoughts, feelings, and behaviors rooted in love.

Bring your journal, pen, computer, and curiosity to learn how to establish these healthier practices. Applying this new knowledge will take courage and persistence to facilitate the transitions and transformations necessary to optimize your Personal Heart Power. The choices are yours to make.

Strengthening Your Personal Heart Power

Practice these tools at your own pace, based on your comfort level, and your ability to practice the tools in the moment. Be patient with yourself as you discover more of your authentic self. These tools are not meant to be single use. Rather, they are tools to be used regularly as needed, strengthened by practice, to maintain or shift into the Mode of Love. Expect moments of challenge, resistance, and discomfort, as well as moments of ease, grace, and accomplishment. The more you practice the tools to open your Personal Heart to Unconditional Love, the easier it will be for you to see meaning in *ALL* of life's experiences, even those that are challenging. You will learn that uncomfortable transition points can also be a welcome gateway to a beautiful transformation—to your new loving way of being in the world.

Chapter 14 is an overall assessment of your Personal Heart in the moment it is taken. This assessment is your guide to determining which tools may be beneficial to explore first. Chapters 15 through 17 are tools for the individual aspects of the Personal Heart. Chapter 18 introduces Universal Tools intended for any Personal Heart State. The remaining chapters present tools for use in each specific Personal

Heart State. If you try a specific tool and find it to be ineffective, try a tool from a different Personal Heart State. Remember, you can use many of the Personal Heart Tools to support the connection between your Personal Heart and calm mind. Only by using them will you discover which tools work most effectively for you and when to use them. Add all the tools that are beneficial to you to your Personal Heart Power Toolbox. With practice, these tools will become second nature to help you build and maintain your Personal Heart Power. Let the Personal Heart Power Tools training begin!

CHAPTER 14

Personal Heart Assessment Tool

The Personal Heart Assessment Tool provides an overall evaluation of your Personal Heart Chambers, Pillars, and Functions. It will give you the awareness of your current Personal Heart State.

This tool is important because it offers an initial baseline and insight into your Personal Heart at your current level of awareness. Once you are aware of this, you can then make conscious choices. Use this tool whenever you want to assess your Personal Heart. Your answers may fluctuate each time you take this assessment because they depend upon how you are responding to life's circumstances in any moment. This assessment provides awareness of the various aspects of your Personal Heart and Mode of Operation. Please remember that this is just an assessment. Resist judging the assessment or the results you get from doing it. There are no right or wrong answers. What you learn from this evaluation will give you information to determine what aspects of your Personal Heart need attention. This tool will help you create a plan to support higher vibrational choices to transition your Personal Heart incrementally into the Mode of Love.

Like anything in life, practice increases your skill level and the more you use this tool, the more competent you'll become when using it. With competency comes a greater awareness of what your current Personal Heart State and your Mode of Operation are. And it's this awareness of your Personal Heart State and Mode of Operation that will guide you to select the best tools to help you restore your Personal Heart Power.

This assessment needs a block of time to explore all aspects of the Personal Heart. Find a space where you can be alone and undisturbed. Grab your pen, paper, journal, computer, or any recording process you prefer to use. It is important to record your answers to gather information so you can reflect on and celebrate your progress toward more Personal Heart Power. Your progress occurs when you use the information from this assessment to balance the various aspects of your Personal Heart.

If you cannot answer a question, move on. Do not overthink it. This Assessment Tool has three sections to evaluate: the Personal Heart Chambers, Pillars, and Functions.

When you've completed the assessment, the following chapters will provide a variety of tools to support you as you transition and transform your Personal Heart. You will be able to identify from which Heart State you are currently operating and that awareness will allow you to choose the most beneficial tools for you in this moment.

The Feelings Chart

This Feelings Chart contains a sample list of lower and higher vibrational feelings. Use it to determine your choices throughout this assessment.

Feelings Chart

Lower Vibrational	Higher Vibrational
Afraid	Secure
Angry	Grateful
Anxious	Peaceful
Depressed	Joyful
Disappointed	Hopeful
Guilty	Proud
Helpless	Courageous
Lonely	Content
Overwhelmed	Inspired
Sad	Happy
Stressed	Relaxed
Unlovable	Lovable

The Assessment for the Four Personal Heart Chambers

Sense your feelings in each of your Personal Heart Chambers. For each statement, circle the number that best represents how you are feeling.

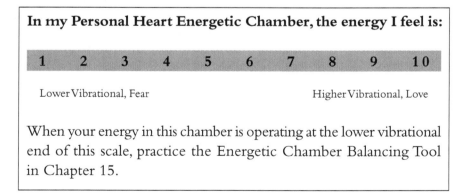

In my Personal Heart Energetic Chamber, the energy I feel is:

1   2   3   4   5   6   7   8   9   10

Lower Vibrational, Fear   Higher Vibrational, Love

When your energy in this chamber is operating at the lower vibrational end of this scale, practice the Energetic Chamber Balancing Tool in Chapter 15.

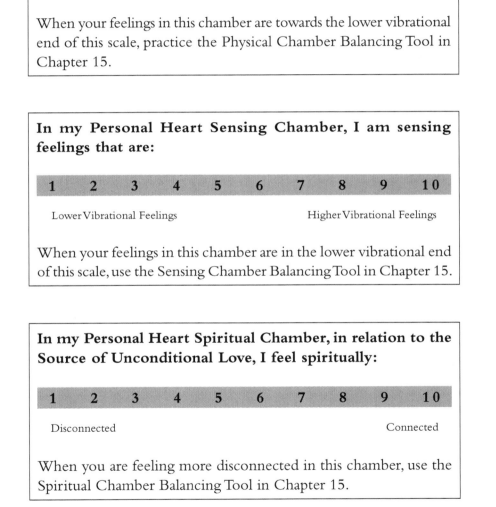

In my Personal Heart Physical Chamber, I feel physically:

| 1 | 2 | 3 | 4 | 5 | 6 | 7 | 8 | 9 | 10 |

Lower Vibrational, Unhealthy   Higher Vibrational, Healthy

When your feelings in this chamber are towards the lower vibrational end of this scale, practice the Physical Chamber Balancing Tool in Chapter 15.

In my Personal Heart Sensing Chamber, I am sensing feelings that are:

| 1 | 2 | 3 | 4 | 5 | 6 | 7 | 8 | 9 | 10 |

Lower Vibrational Feelings   Higher Vibrational Feelings

When your feelings in this chamber are in the lower vibrational end of this scale, use the Sensing Chamber Balancing Tool in Chapter 15.

In my Personal Heart Spiritual Chamber, in relation to the Source of Unconditional Love, I feel spiritually:

| 1 | 2 | 3 | 4 | 5 | 6 | 7 | 8 | 9 | 10 |

Disconnected   Connected

When you are feeling more disconnected in this chamber, use the Spiritual Chamber Balancing Tool in Chapter 15.

The Assessment for the Four Personal Heart Pillars

In this section of the assessment, evaluate the strength of each of your Personal Heart Pillars.

In my Personal Heart Presence Pillar, my ability to be present in the moment is:

1	2	3	4	5	6	7	8	9	10

Non-supportive, Challenging   Very Supportive, Easy

When this pillar is less supportive, practice the Presence Pillar Balancing Tool in Chapter 16.

In my Personal Heart Safety Pillar, I currently feel:

1	2	3	4	5	6	7	8	9	10

Non-supportive, Unsafe   Very Supportive, Safe

When this pillar is less supportive, use the Safety Pillar Balancing Tool in Chapter 16.

In my Personal Heart Unconditional Love Pillar, my sense of connection to the Source of Unconditional Love is:

1	2	3	4	5	6	7	8	9	10

Non-supportive, Disconnected   Very Supportive, Connected

When this pillar is less supportive, practice the Unconditional Love Pillar Balancing Tool in Chapter 16.

In my Personal Heart Community Pillar, my connection to community feels:

1	2	3	4	5	6	7	8	9	10

Non-supportive Community   Very Supportive Community

When this pillar is less supportive, use the Community Pillar Balancing Tool in Chapter 16.

The Assessment for the Four Personal Heart Functions

For this section of the assessment, use your perception to determine how you are operating from lower to higher vibrational energy in your four Personal Heart Functions. Recognizing when you are functioning from the lower vibrational energies allows you to choose the tools to support your transition back into the higher vibrational energies for each Personal Heart Function.

In my Personal Heart Taking Function, I sense I am primarily taking in energy that is:

1	2	3	4	5	6	7	8	9	10

Lower Vibrational   Higher Vibrational

When you find yourself in lower vibrational energies in the Taking Function, use the Taking Function Balancing Tool in Chapter 17.

In my Personal Heart Dismissing Function, I sense I am dismissing energy that is:

(**Note** reversed continuum: dismissing higher vibrational energy is a lower vibrational behavior, therefore, a one on the continuum. Dismissing lower vibrational energy is a higher vibrational behavior therefore, a ten on the continuum.)

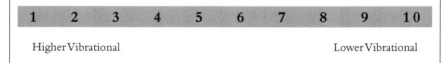

1	2	3	4	5	6	7	8	9	10

Higher Vibrational   Lower Vibrational

When you find yourself in lower vibrational energies in the Dismissing Function, use the Dismissing Function Balancing Tool in Chapter 17.

In my Personal Heart Giving Function, I sense I am primarily giving out energy that is:

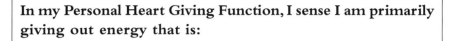

1	2	3	4	5	6	7	8	9	10

Lower Vibrational   Higher Vibrational

When you find yourself in lower vibrational energies in the Giving Function, use the Giving Function Balancing Tool in Chapter 17.

In my Personal Heart Withholding Function, I sense I am primarily withholding energy that is:

(**Note** reversed continuum: withholding higher vibrational energy is a lower vibrational behavior, therefore, a one on the continuum. Withholding lower vibrational energy is a higher vibrational behavior therefore, a ten on the continuum.)

1	2	3	4	5	6	7	8	9	10

Higher Vibrational   Lower Vibrational

When you find yourself in the lower vibrational energies in the Withholding Function, use the Withholding Function Balancing Tool in Chapter 17.

The Personal Heart Assessment Chart

To get the most from this assessment, fill in the chart below by circling the number that corresponds to what you circled in the assessment for each aspect of your Personal Heart. The numbers circled allow you to see a snapshot of the range of the vibrational energies you are operating from in your Personal Heart. This awareness will provide information for determining your Personal Heart State in this moment, enabling you to choose the appropriate tools.

Personal Heart Assessment Tool

Aspects of Personal Heart	Vibrational Energy Continuum (lower to higher)									
Physical Chamber	1	2	3	4	5	6	7	8	9	10
Sensing Chamber (feelings)	1	2	3	4	5	6	7	8	9	10
Energetic Chamber	1	2	3	4	5	6	7	8	9	10
Spiritual Chamber	1	2	3	4	5	6	7	8	9	10
Presence Pillar	1	2	3	4	5	6	7	8	9	10
Safety Pillar	1	2	3	4	5	6	7	8	9	10
Unconditional LOVE Pillar	1	2	3	4	5	6	7	8	9	10
Community Pillar	1	2	3	4	5	6	7	8	9	10
Taking Function	1	2	3	4	5	6	7	8	9	10
Dismissing Function*	1	2	3	4	5	6	7	8	9	10
Giving Function	1	2	3	4	5	6	7	8	9	10
Withholding Function*	1	2	3	4	5	6	7	8	9	10
Total no. circled in each column										
Mode of Operation	Fear	F	F	F	F	L	L	L	L	Love
Personal Heart States	Disc.	Reactive		Half-Hearted			Content		Whole	

*Remember the continuum for the Dismissing and Withholding Functions is reversed.

Notice in your chart the numbers you have circled and the range you are operating from in each aspect of the Personal Heart. Look with curiosity, not judgment, at which aspects are between one and five, and which are between six and ten. If most of your circled numbers are five or below, then this suggests you are currently operating primarily from the Mode of Fear. Whereas, if most of your numbers are six and higher, the Mode of Love is likely your current primary Mode of Operation. This overview gives you some insight as to which aspects of your Personal Heart need loving attention.

You are now at a Choice Point to decide if you will use this information to implement tools that can increase your Personal Heart Power or not. You may feel satisfied with your life right now and don't feel a need to change anything. However, when you have a desire to increase your Personal Heart Power, you receive the most benefit by beginning with the aspects with the lowest numbers. Chapters 15 through 17 contain tools for rebalancing the Personal Heart Chambers, Pillars, and Functions, respectively. It is about feeling compassion for yourself, no matter what you choose to do at this time.

Another way to use this chart is to determine your Personal Heart State. To do this, notice the range of numbers you have circled. Typically, the vibrational energy range is where you have most numbers circled. The numbers in the chart represent the five Personal Heart States and their different vibrational energy ranges:

1   =   Disconnected Heart State
2-3   =   Reactive Heart State
4-7   =   Half-hearted Heart State
8-9   =   Content Heart State
10   =   Whole Heart State

Knowing your Personal Heart State is another way to determine which Personal Heart Power Tools to use to support your shift into higher vibrational energies for a more love-focused life. Shifting to higher vibrational energies in the various aspects of your Personal Heart will help you transition towards the Mode of Love. To remind yourself of what each Personal Heart State is, refer to the glossary at the end of this book.

The following chapters provide tools for each aspect of the Personal Heart, Universal Tools, and specific tools for each Personal Heart State. It is best to practice tools that correlate to the individual aspects with the lowest vibrational numbers or specific tools designed for your current Personal Heart State.

CHAPTER 15

Tools for the Four Personal Heart Chambers

In this chapter, use the information from the Personal Heart Assessment Tool to determine which Chamber Tools would be most beneficial for you at this time.

The Energetic Chamber Balancing Tool

The Energetic Chamber Balancing Tool balances your energetic flow so you can operate in the Mode of Love more frequently. The Energetic Chamber controls the vibrational flow of energy housed by the Personal Heart and mind. It fuels the range of lower to higher vibrational thoughts and feelings. A depletion in energy can result from a variety of reasons. By intentionally creating awareness, you will be able to implement changes that create more balance in your Energetic Chamber.

Practice

Take a quick awareness assessment:

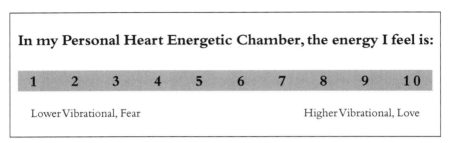

In my Personal Heart Energetic Chamber, the energy I feel is:

1	2	3	4	5	6	7	8	9	10

Lower Vibrational, Fear   Higher Vibrational, Love

Having this personal awareness of your energetic level allows you to discover what you need to transition towards operating with a higher vibrational energy level. With an answer of five or less, practicing this tool will help you raise your vibrational level. With an answer of six or more, this tool is supportive in maintaining the Mode of Love.

1. With that awareness, make a list of what you believe contributes to you operating with lower vibrational energy or what is keeping you from operating with higher vibrational energy. Some examples are:

    °   not enough sleep,
    °   stressful situations,
    °   working long hours.

2. With your list, determine what higher vibrational thoughts, feelings, and behaviors you can implement to balance your Personal Heart Energetic Chamber:

    °   *The higher vibrational **thoughts** I can think of now to raise my energetic level are:*

    o   *The higher vibrational **feelings** I can feel now to raise my energetic level are:*

    o   *The higher vibrational **behaviors** I can do now to raise my energetic level are:*

3. Implement your newly identified higher vibrational thoughts, feelings, and behaviors, and observe and record any change in your Energetic Chamber.
4. Reassess regularly to support your transition to higher vibrational energy for a more balanced Energetic Chamber.

The Physical Chamber Balancing Tool

This tool can help to balance your Personal Heart Physical Chamber. Your body is your physical container. Keeping it in balance helps you to operate from the Mode of Love and feel vibrant in your life. You will want to focus on how to care for your mind and body to create healthy limits that are beneficial and loving for you.

Physical balance is not about being *perfect*, but about taking care of your body's needs and keeping it in balance throughout the day the best you can. Aiming for abstract perfection often creates Stress Loops from the Mode of Fear with stressful beliefs and unhealthy limits. These will either keep the body under rigid control or under no control, creating a lack of self-care.

To re-establish balance in your Personal Heart Physical Chamber, you need to create an awareness of what you need to focus on to have physical balance. The upcoming list will help.

Practice

Take a quick awareness assessment:

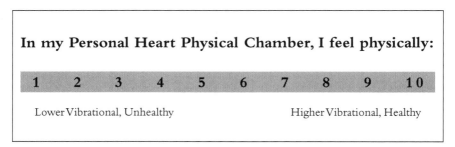

In my Personal Heart Physical Chamber, I feel physically:

1	2	3	4	5	6	7	8	9	10

Lower Vibrational, Unhealthy   Higher Vibrational, Healthy

Look at the six main categories for balance in the Personal Heart Physical Chamber and determine where you feel there is a need for attention. Each one is followed by ideas that may support your desire to have balance in your Personal Heart Physical Chamber, shifting you from the Mode of Fear to the Mode of Love.

1. Sleep

Create a healthy bedtime routine by thinking consciously of what might be prohibiting your sleep and taking steps to change it. Some common sleep zappers and solutions include:

- Poor quality sleeping environment: create an environment that supports sleep through comfort, lack of distractions, and safety.
- Inconsistency: create a consistent bedtime routine.
- Stimulants: eliminate caffeine, nicotine, food, late evening exercise, and other sources that are stimulants for you.
- Screen time: eliminate screen time one hour or more before bedtime. In reality, any amount of screen time eliminated before bedtime is beneficial.

2. Healthy Nutrition

What you eat or don't eat really matters. Everyone needs a well-balanced, nutritional eating pattern. However, well-balanced and nutritional can mean different things for different people.

- Develop a nutritional eating pattern that suits your body's needs.
- Eat the highest quality food available to you.
- Eat the quantity of food that keeps your body in optimal physical health.

3. Physical Activity

Determine what you need for optimal health in the present moment. Create a healthy balance in your daily physical activity by including body movement of any kind. Some examples are:

- walking,
- dancing,
- yoga,
- tai chi,
- exercise,
- sports,
- physical labor, such as:
  - mowing the lawn,
  - planting and maintaining a garden,
  - raking leaves,
  - cleaning your house.

It is also possible to do too much physical activity, which can be as counterproductive to your health as doing nothing.

4. Health Care

Look after yourself by arranging and attending annual check-ups or physicals. Regularly take medication, supplements, or vitamins necessary for healthy physical support. Listen to your body when it speaks through ongoing pain or discomfort and seek health care support when needed.

5. Self-nurturing Care

Take care of yourself by doing some of the following:

- walk or play in nature,
- nurture your body with a massage, bubble baths, lotions, self-hugs, hugs from others,
- express loving, higher vibrational statements to your body,
- build a healthy relationship with your body,
- spend time with *feel-good* people: those you care about and who care about you.

6. Mental Health Care

Mental health is just as important as physical health. We all need mental health support with additional support in stressful times. Do what you need to do for balance in the five previous points, and then:

- Build a strong community support system:
  - family,
  - friends,
  - work,
  - organizations,
  - support groups.
- Seek therapeutic support from professionals:
  - counselors,
  - coaches,
  - therapists,

     ◦   social workers,

     ◦   doctors.

Looking at each of these six categories:

1. List the categories where you feel you would benefit from changing some of your current behaviors.
2. For each category listed, list one or two things you could implement now to engage those behaviors that will allow you to create more balance in your Personal Heart Physical Chamber.
3. Pay attention to which behavior changes benefit you, and make them a part of your routine.
4. Continue to make incremental changes when necessary.
5. Recognize, honor, and celebrate your physical and mental health.

With your awareness, implement a plan that supports your transition in a way that is realistic and possible to incorporate for the long-term gains. Trying to do everything, or too much, at one time may hold you back from success. It is better to begin slowly. As you make some progress, you are more likely to add other changes later. If something doesn't work, try something else. Not all things work for all people. Decide what you can do now and implement it. Ideally, track your physical changes in your journal, or by utilizing the Personal Heart Assessment Tool over time, to gain as much awareness as possible. Remember to recognize and honor your progress to your Personal Heart Physical Chamber's well-being.

The Sensing Chamber Balancing Tool

The Sensing Chamber Balancing Tool guides you to discover your feelings, assess these feelings, and process through the lower vibrational ones so you can more accurately determine your needs. This tool can be most beneficial when you are overreacting and overthinking the little things in life. These overreactions indicate unexpressed feelings that have built up.

Imbalance in your Personal Heart Sensing Chamber occurs from an unmet need or an unfelt feeling that needs processing. To re-establish balance in your Personal Heart Sensing Chamber, it is beneficial to notice why you are having lower vibrational feelings so you can accept or process through them to higher vibrational feelings.

Practice

Take a quick awareness assessment:

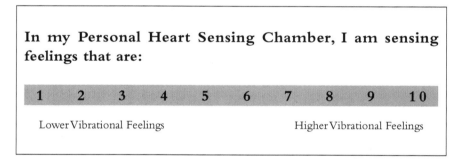

In my Personal Heart Sensing Chamber, I am sensing feelings that are:

1	2	3	4	5	6	7	8	9	10

Lower Vibrational Feelings   Higher Vibrational Feelings

Become aware and acknowledge the feelings you are feeling in this moment. Use the Feelings Chart when you need support to determine your feelings. Record them in your journal as a record of your journey. Why you are having these feelings will not necessarily arise in the moment. Be aware the reason could present itself later. This information is beneficial for your processing because it can add clarity to what is needed to re-establish balance in this chamber. Sometimes just acknowledging the feelings can shift this chamber back to balance.

For example, your child moves to another town, and you are excited about their opportunity. Practicing this tool, you discover a feeling of sadness. While breathing, you realize you feel sad because your child has moved away. This awareness allows for acceptance as you hold both the excitement and sadness.

The Feelings Diagram

Lower Vibrational	Higher Vibrational
Afraid	Secure
Angry	Grateful
Anxious	Peaceful
Depressed	Joyful
Disappointed	Hopeful
Guilty	Proud
Helpless	Courageous
Lonely	Content
Overwhelmed	Inspired
Sad	Happy
Stressed	Relaxed
Unlovable	Lovable

The lower vibrational **feelings** *I feel in my Personal Heart Sensing Chamber are...*

The higher vibrational **feelings** *I feel in my Personal Heart Sensing Chamber are...*

1. After identifying the feelings, begin by consciously feeling each lower vibrational feeling, one at a time, while breathing slowly and deeply.
2. While breathing, do any thoughts arise as to why you are having this feeling?

3. With that thought, are you able to understand the feeling and choose to accept or release that feeling?

4. When you can accept or release the feeling, sense if you feel more balanced. If you do, move on to the next lower vibrational feeling and repeat the process. If not, continue.

When you can't identify why you have a feeling, use supportive thoughts and behaviors to help process through it.

- *My lower vibrational feeling is…*
- *What this feeling is telling me I need now is…*
- *What higher vibrational behavior can I do to take care of this feeling?*
- Implement the behavior. Evaluate its effectiveness in rebalancing your feeling. The amount of time varies depending on the intensity of the feeling.
- Repeat as needed for other lower vibrational feelings.

When you need more support for rebalancing in this Personal Heart Chamber, use one or more of the following tools:

- Thought Awareness Tool in Chapter 18,
- Reassurance Tool in Chapter 19,
- Shift Tool in Chapter 20,
- Tools for your current Personal Heart State in Chapters 19-23.

The Spiritual Chamber Balancing Tool

The Spiritual Chamber Balancing Tool allows you to maintain and develop spiritual practices that support your connection to the Source of Unconditional Love.

Practice

Take a quick awareness assessment:

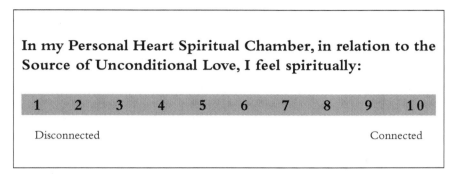

In my Personal Heart Spiritual Chamber, in relation to the Source of Unconditional Love, I feel spiritually:

| 1 | 2 | 3 | 4 | 5 | 6 | 7 | 8 | 9 | 10 |

Disconnected   Connected

Use this information to help you identify what you need to become aware of in your connection to the Source of Unconditional Love. If you desire more awareness of a loving connection with the Source of Unconditional Love, begin implementing more loving practices.

Here is a list of some loving practices that might enhance your awareness of connection to the Source of Unconditional Love in the Spiritual Chamber:

- prayer,
- meditation,
- spiritual and religious communities,
- higher vibrational music,
- retreats and workshops,
- books,
- coaching.

Other tools that may be beneficial for balancing the Spiritual Chamber are:

- Meditation Tool in Chapter 18.
- Soul Moments Tool in Chapter 18.
- Higher Vibrational Affirmation Tool in Chapter 18.
- Love Moments Tool in Chapter 22.
- Whole Heart Tool in Chapter 23.

Have fun finding other tools to support you on your journey to a more balanced Personal Heart Spiritual Chamber. As you begin your practice, notice how your relationship with life feels more love-focused, even when your external circumstances may not have changed.

CHAPTER 16

Tools for the Four Personal Heart Pillars

The four Personal Heart Pillars create the stability of your Personal Heart. By consciously monitoring the pillars' stability, you can determine which tools might serve you best to improve their strength.

The Presence Pillar Balancing Tool

The Presence Pillar Balancing Tool aims to develop the ability to stay focused in the present moment. Being present allows things that are not relevant to your current situation to be set aside, knowing you can return to them when they are relevant. These quick-to-implement tools can be useful when you feel challenged to stay in the present moment, and they will help you identify what is *pulling you out* of it. This knowledge will enable you to make beneficial choices to create a more supportive Presence Pillar and help you decide whether to stay in the present moment or intentionally switch to what is taking your attention now.

Practice

Take a quick awareness assessment:

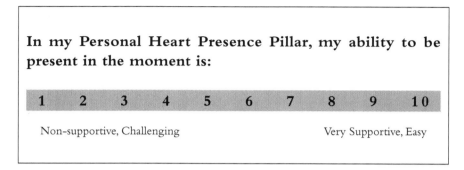

In my Personal Heart Presence Pillar, my ability to be present in the moment is:

1	2	3	4	5	6	7	8	9	10

Non-supportive, Challenging   Very Supportive, Easy

Conscious Breathing Practice

This breathing practice engages the parasympathetic nervous system, which calms your mind and strengthens your Presence Pillar. Focusing on breathing reduces distractions in your mind and reconnects you to the simplicity of your breath. With a less-distracted mind, it becomes easier to choose what you want to focus on.

1. Take three slow, deep breaths.
    *   Ideally, allow five seconds for each inhale, slowly breathing deeply into your lower abdomen, and for each exhale, slowly releasing the breath.
    *   Focus on the inhale and exhale of each breath throughout the cycle.
2. Do you feel more present after the breathing cycle? If not, repeat this cycle several more times.
3. If you still find yourself distracted from the present moment, try one, or both, of the following tools.

Recentering Practice

This is a practice to shift from lower vibrational and distracting thoughts back into the present moment by literally stating your current situation:

"In this moment, I am just a person who is…" (e.g.: sitting in my living room, walking outside, attending a meeting, etc.)

Repeat this statement several times until you feel yourself back in the present moment. The simplicity of the literal statement allows you to return to the present moment and eliminate the distractions of all your thoughts.

Journaling Practice

This is a stream of consciousness journaling in which you write with the flow of your thoughts without judging or editing them. Sit with your journal, computer, or paper, and literally write everything flowing through your mind. Write without editing, or worrying about sentence structure, punctuation, or grammar. The free flow process is what is important. What you write provides insights into which thoughts are distracting you from the present moment. The awareness allows you to make choices:

- Let go of the distracting thoughts and remain in the present moment.
- Choose a behavior to take care of the distracting thought, so you can return to the current situation with a less distracted mind.

The Safety Pillar Balancing Tool

The Safety Pillar Balancing Tool helps to develop awareness and a skill set to create a sense of safety for yourself. This is about feeling secure physically and emotionally in any situation, trusting that no harm will be done to you. To gain awareness of your present perception of safety, there are two things to consider.

1. Physical Safety

Physical safety is when you feel your physical body is safe from harm wherever you are. If you do not feel safe, make it a practice to take action to minimize and preferably eliminate the potentially harmful risk.

2. Emotional Safety

Emotional safety is when you feel safe to express your full range of feelings effectively in a particular situation. This is when you can discern whether you are feeling safe in the situation to express your feelings or if it is safer for you to withhold them. This discernment is creating emotional safety for yourself.

A lack of emotional safety can arise from lower vibrational judgments, feelings, and behaviors from yourself or others.

Practice

Take a quick awareness assessment:

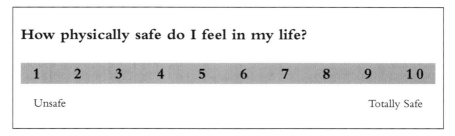

How physically safe do I feel in my life?

| 1 | 2 | 3 | 4 | 5 | 6 | 7 | 8 | 9 | 10 |

Unsafe   Totally Safe

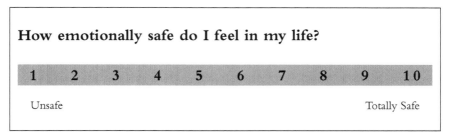

How emotionally safe do I feel in my life?

| 1 | 2 | 3 | 4 | 5 | 6 | 7 | 8 | 9 | 10 |

Unsafe   Totally Safe

With this awareness, decide if you would like to make your life physically or emotionally safer. Go through the following practice to support creating more safety in your life.

Physical or Emotional Safety

1. If your numbers are optimal for you, enjoy your physical or emotional safety. If one or both are not optimal, continue this practice. Go through the practice for physical and emotional safety separately.
2. List all the reasons you do not feel physically/emotionally safe.
3. For each reason you feel unsafe, list ideas that could create more physical/emotional safety for you. When it is too challenging to think of ideas, reach out for support.
4. To create safety, you will need to choose to implement the ideas that will create your physical/emotional safety.
5. As you implement your ideas, assess if you feel more physically/emotionally safe. When you do, determine if there are any other steps needed to increase safety. If not, then thoroughly enjoy and appreciate feeling safe.
6. When you continue to feel unsafe, you may need additional support to determine how you can strengthen your physical/emotional safety.

Some ideas to rebalance your Safety Pillar are:
- setting healthy limits with yourself,
- setting healthy boundaries with others,
- removing yourself from unsafe situations,
- creating or taking part in situations that you feel safe in,
- developing awareness of safety,
- trusting yourself to keep yourself safe,
- reaching out for safety support.

If this tool conjures up feelings that need processing through, the Sensing Chamber Balancing Tool, the Universal Tools, or tools for your current Personal Heart State may offer more support. If you feel significantly emotionally stressed, it is often beneficial to seek additional support from a group or private counselor specializing in emotional issues.

The Unconditional Love Pillar Balancing Tool

The Unconditional Love Pillar Balancing Tool creates and maintains a strong connection to the energetic glue that connects you to your Personal Heart. This loving energy supports your connection to yourself, others, and the world. Unconditional Love is a higher vibrational energy that is often challenging to hold. Any work done on the Unconditional Love Pillar is valuable for yourself and for maintaining Personal Heart Power.

Practice

Take a quick awareness assessment:

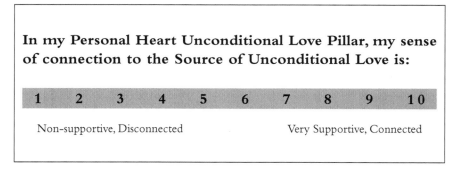

With this awareness, decide if you would like to feel more supported with Unconditional Love. Some Personal Heart Power Tools that can be supportive of the Unconditional Love Pillar are:

- Heart Hugs Tool in Chapter 18,
- Soul Moments Tool in Chapter 18,
- Love Moments Tool in Chapter 22,
- Whole Heart Tool in Chapter 23.

Any time you love yourself, others, and the world, you are stabilizing, strengthening, and balancing your Personal Heart Unconditional Love Pillar. Making choices that support this pillar makes a love-focused life happen.

The Community Pillar Balancing Tool

The Personal Heart Community Pillar is the stabilizer of your Personal Heart in relationship with others. You are meant to be loved, valued, seen, heard, and respected when taking part in relationships and communities. When possible, intentionally choose people and communities who fuel your Personal Heart Power lovingly.

Practice

Take a quick awareness assessment:

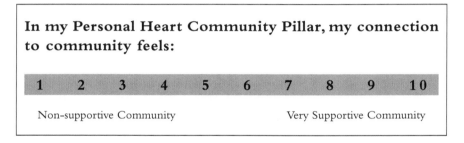

In my Personal Heart Community Pillar, my connection to community feels:

| 1 | 2 | 3 | 4 | 5 | 6 | 7 | 8 | 9 | 10 |

Non-supportive Community   Very Supportive Community

With this awareness, it is beneficial to determine where the weaker areas are in your Community Pillar:

1. Make a list of all the ways you are connected to people.
   - Individuals—friends, family, co-workers, neighbors, and others with whom you associate.
   - Groups—social, organizations, co-workers, board, education, and other groups with which you are involved.
2. Access on the continuum for each person or group, how connected and supported you feel by them.

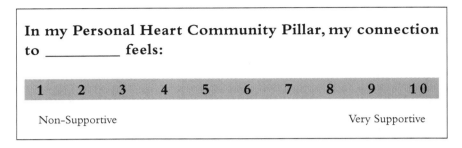

In my Personal Heart Community Pillar, my connection to _____ feels:

| 1 | 2 | 3 | 4 | 5 | 6 | 7 | 8 | 9 | 10 |

Non-Supportive   Very Supportive

This information provides an awareness of which people or groups are enhancing your love-focused life and which are making it more challenging. You can now consciously discern what you would like to do with this information. Remember, some people who are challenging us are there to teach us valuable lessons.

To rebalance your Community Pillar:
1. Determine which relationships and communities you feel supported in. Implement a practice to maintain them and offer gratitude for them.
2. Determine which relationships and communities you feel less supported in. For each of these:
    a) Discern why it doesn't feel supportive. Is there anything about it that feels supportive?
    b) Is there anything you can do to make this relationship or community more supportive? (e.g., say what you need, do not need, or request more support.)
    c) If there is no sense of support, discern if you want to let go of the relationship or community.
    d) Follow through with your intentions and re-evaluate as needed.

Making changes to create a life that enhances your opportunity to be involved with more loving and supportive people and communities strengthens your Community Pillar. If you do not have the community support you want, join a community with similar interests to you. Some ways you can expand and strengthen your Community Pillar are:

- making choices to reduce or eliminate the time you spend with the relationships or groups where you do not feel supported in your Community Pillar,
- taking classes you would enjoy (e.g., educational, yoga, dance, writing, cooking, etc.),
- joining supportive religious and spiritual groups,
- joining clubs (book, movie, sports, cooking, social club, collectors' clubs, etc.),
- seeking new employment,
- learning how to communicate more effectively in personal relationships and communities.

CHAPTER 17

Tools for the Four Personal Heart Functions

The Personal Heart Functions Tools create optimal functioning within the Personal Heart. Recognizing when you are functioning from lower or higher vibrational energies will allow you to select and practice these tools, as well as other tools that will support optimal performance in your Personal Heart. For each Personal Heart Function Tool, you can answer the assessment from an overall Personal Heart perspective or for a specific relationship or community.

Remember, the Personal Heart States are on a continuum:

1	=	Disconnected,
2 & 3	=	Reactive,
4, 5, 6, & 7	=	Half-hearted,
8 & 9	=	Content,
10	=	Whole.

Practice the tools for each of the four functions: Taking, Dismissing, Giving, and Withholding. If you want more tools to support your functioning from the Mode of Love, visit the Universal Tools or the tools for your specific Personal Heart State in this moment.

The Taking Function Balancing Tool

Take a quick awareness assessment:

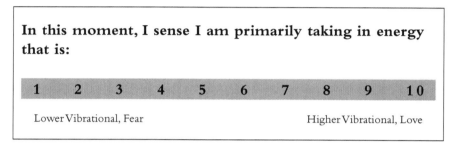

In this moment, I sense I am primarily taking in energy that is:

1	2	3	4	5	6	7	8	9	10

Lower Vibrational, Fear   Higher Vibrational, Love

This information offers awareness. Five and below shows you are operating more from the Mode of Fear and six or higher indicates you are operating more from the Mode of Love. Choose the steps you would like to take to increase the vibrational quality and quantity of your Taking Function.

To shift to taking in higher vibrational energy from ourselves or others:

1. Make a list of where and when you are taking in lower vibrational energy (e.g., thoughts, feelings, and behaviors from ourselves or others; feeling depleted after being with someone), and then:

   a. Implement higher vibrational thoughts that you can use to take in the higher vibrational energy through your Taking Function. For additional support, use the Thought Awareness Tool in Chapter 18.

    b.   Process through lower vibrational feelings so you do not take in the lower vibrational energy. For additional support, use the Sensing Chamber Balancing Tool in Chapter 15.

    c.   Implement higher vibrational behaviors that can support taking in higher vibrational energies. For additional support, use the Balancing Behaviors Tool in Chapter 21.

2.   Reassess your Taking Function on the continuum to see if the quality and quantity of the energy you are taking in has shifted to taking in higher vibrational energies while staying in balance.

The Dismissing Function Balancing Tool

Take a quick awareness assessment:

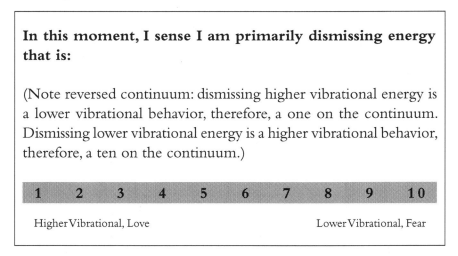

In this moment, I sense I am primarily dismissing energy that is:

(Note reversed continuum: dismissing higher vibrational energy is a lower vibrational behavior, therefore, a one on the continuum. Dismissing lower vibrational energy is a higher vibrational behavior, therefore, a ten on the continuum.)

1	2	3	4	5	6	7	8	9	10

Higher Vibrational, Love   Lower Vibrational, Fear

This information offers awareness. You are in the Mode of Fear when dismissing higher vibrational energies, and in the Mode of Love when you dismiss lower vibrational energies. Choose the steps you would like to take to dismiss the lower vibrational energies to increase the vibrational quality of what you take into your Personal Heart.

To shift to dismissing lower vibrational energy:
1. Make a list of where and when you are dismissing higher vibrational energy (e.g., compliments, loving support of yourself and from others), and then:
    a. Implement higher vibrational thoughts to dismiss lower vibrational thoughts to shift to the Mode of Love in your Dismissing Function. For additional support, use the Thought Awareness Tool in Chapter 18.
    b. Process through your lower vibrational feelings so you can dismiss them and shift into higher vibrational feelings. For additional support, use the Sensing Chamber Balancing Tool in Chapter 15.
    c. Implement higher vibrational behaviors that would help support dismissing lower vibrational energies. For additional support, use the Balancing Behaviors Tool in Chapter 21.
2. Reassess your Dismissing Function on the continuum to see if you are dismissing more lower vibrational energies while staying in balance.

The Giving Function Balancing Tool

Take a quick awareness assessment:

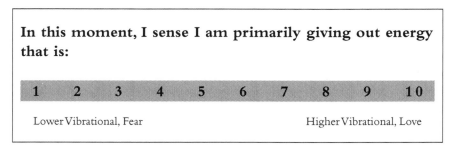

In this moment, I sense I am primarily giving out energy that is:

1	2	3	4	5	6	7	8	9	10

Lower Vibrational, Fear   Higher Vibrational, Love

This information offers more awareness so you can choose the steps you would like to take to increase the vibrational quality and quantity of your Giving Function.

To shift to giving out higher vibrational energy:

1. Make a list of where and when you are giving out lower vibrational energies (e.g., judgmental comments, gossiping, sarcasm, gifts out of obligation).

    a. Implement higher vibrational thoughts to replace your lower vibrational thoughts and shift to higher vibrational energies in your Giving Function. For additional support, use the Thought Awareness Tool in Chapter 18.

    b. Process through any lower vibrational feelings so you can give out higher vibrational energies. For additional support, use the Sensing Chamber Balancing Tool in Chapter 15.

    c. Implement higher vibrational behaviors that can support giving out higher vibrational energy. For additional support, use the Balancing Behaviors Tool in Chapter 21.

2. Reassess your Giving Function on the continuum to see if you are giving out higher vibrational energies while staying in balance.

The Withholding Function Balancing Tool

Take a quick awareness assessment:

In this moment, I sense I am primarily withholding energy that is:

(Note reversed continuum: withholding higher vibrational energy is a lower vibrational behavior, therefore, a one on the continuum. Withholding lower vibrational energy is a higher vibrational behavior, therefore, a ten on the continuum.)

1	2	3	4	5	6	7	8	9	10

Higher Vibrational, Love   Lower Vibrational, Fear

Understand that withholding higher vibrational energy is typically from the Mode of Fear and withholding the lower vibrational energy is from the Mode of Love. In the Mode of Fear, withholding is triggered by the fear of rejection, ridicule, painful consequences, and other fear-based beliefs. In the Mode of Love, withholding is motivated by the love for others, because you do not want to cause pain, and the love for yourself so you can remain in higher vibrational energies and balance. With this awareness, choose the steps you would like to take to shift into the Mode of Love in your Withholding Function.

To shift to withholding from the Mode of Love:

1. Make a list of where and when you are withholding lower and higher vibrational energies, and then:

    a. For each item on your list, determine if you are withholding from the Mode of Fear or the Mode of Love. For additional support, use the Thought Awareness Tool in Chapter 18.

    b. Determine how withholding makes you feel and process through the lower vibrational feelings. For additional support, use the Sensing Chamber Balancing Tool in Chapter 15.

    c. Implement higher vibrational behaviors that support withholding lower vibrational energy from the Mode of Love. For additional support, use the Balancing Behaviors Tool in Chapter 21.

2. Reassess your Withholding Function on the continuum to see if you are withholding vibrational energies from the Mode of Love.

CHAPTER 18

Universal Tools

We now offer a selection of Universal Tools that may help you on your Personal Heart Power Journey. As you explore these, sense which ones are most beneficial and effective for you and add them to your Personal Heart Power Toolbox. You can use these tools for multiple Personal Heart States and, remember, do not use the information to judge yourself. Rather, use the information to gain awareness of yourself as you are transitioning into a more love-focused life.

The Mode Check-in Tool

The Mode Check-in Tool provides a conscious way to determine if you are operating from the Mode of Fear or the Mode of Love in the present moment and over a period of time. You will become aware of whether your thoughts, feelings, and behaviors are energized by Fear or Love. Challenge yourself to check-in several times throughout the day to see if your Mode of Operation changes. If so, consider why this may be. Once you're aware, you can make the conscious choice to shift towards the Mode of Love. Please be gentle with yourself. You are gathering more awareness and information about your Personal

Heart's Mode of Operation. Think of this inventory as a data-gathering adventure. How you use this data will unfold in the pages to come.

Practice

Grab your pen and paper or whatever recording process you prefer to use.

Use the Mode Check-in Chart provided or create a table with four columns and enough rows for you to record information several times throughout the day. We recommend at least five. Do this for at least one week. Each time you check in throughout the day, make a quick note of what is happening in the moment and note whether you're operating from the Mode of Love or the Mode of Fear. Record this information on the table. Doing this over a period of time gives you an insight into when you are operating from the Mode of Fear or the Mode of Love. This awareness gives information to support your choices for a more love-focused life.

The Mode Check-In Chart

Check-In	Mode of Operation (Circle one)	Date	Time	Why did you choose this Mode now?
#1	Fear or Love			
#2	Fear or Love			
#3	Fear or Love			
#4	Fear or Love			
#5	Fear or Love			

At the end of the week, review your observations and see which Mode you operated from most often. Whenever you are operating from the Mode of Fear, use the tools that will help you shift into the Mode of Love. And when you are operating from the Mode of Love, continue with any practices that keep you in this Mode of Operation.

If you find yourself challenged to check-in, here are some suggestions that might make it easier:

- Set a specific time of day to check-in, such as when you wake up, at mealtimes, or before bed.
- Set a timer.
- Find a friend to check in with for accountability.

Find what works best for you to create and maintain a consistent routine.

The Thought Awareness Tool

The Thought Awareness Tool's purpose is to provide you with information regarding the vibrational quality of your thoughts in the present moment and how you can shift the vibrational quality of those thoughts if needed. Knowledge is power. This information will help you know what is on your mind.

Thoughts are not meant to be judged. They help you gather information on the status of your mind, body functioning, and your surrounding. The chaotic mind is typically driven by lower vibrational thoughts, which can include the *what-ifs, should-haves, always, nevers, I hate,* and *I can't.* The calm mind is driven by higher vibrational thoughts, which can include *possibilities, haves, likely, I love,* and *I can.* Being aware of this information allows you to recognize the difference between lower and higher vibrational thoughts and choose to shift to higher vibrational thoughts more frequently.

Practice

Grab your pen and paper or whatever recording process you prefer to use.

1. Find a quiet and comfortable space where you won't be disturbed for about ten minutes.

2. Set a timer on your phone or watch for five minutes.

3. Start the timer.

4. Using a list format, write down every thought running through your mind for the next five minutes.

5. Do not think about, analyze, or judge what you're writing. Don't worry about grammar or punctuation. Just write.

6. When the timer goes off, go back to each thought in your list and mark whether the thought is higher vibrational, lower vibrational, or if you're unsure.

7. Next, look at the thoughts you marked as lower vibrational and see if you can easily release them from your mind.

8. If you can release them, simply cross them out. This represents letting go of these thoughts. Feel the power in setting a healthy limit with your mind by letting go of your lower vibrational thoughts.

9. If that doesn't work, try to change the thought to be higher vibrational in nature. For example, do you remember the floral treasures we bought for our dream home where we judged ourselves and wondered how we could have been so stupid and irresponsible for letting the plants dry out in the sun? Let's shift *stupid and irresponsible* to a higher vibrational thought, such as, *It's okay to make mistakes.* Can you see how this language feels more loving?

10. Be compassionate with yourself if you can't let go or shift the lower vibrational thought in the moment. Try to stay present, as best you can, to reduce the intensity of the lower vibrational thought.

11. Next, go to the thoughts you are unsure about. How does each unsure thought make you feel? If you feel higher vibrational feelings, keep the thought. But if you feel lower vibrational feelings, try to let it go or transition the thought into a higher vibrational one.

12. On your paper, cross out the unsure thoughts that you could let go of from your mind.

13. Now, look at your higher vibrational thoughts. Enjoy and recognize the benefits of these thoughts.

14. Check in again to see if your mind feels calmer after letting go of the lower vibrational thoughts and transitioning to higher vibrational thoughts.

If you cannot calm your mind, start with the Meditation Tool that follows next. You can also practice any other mind-focused tools.

The Meditation Tool

Meditation effectively enhances the ability to open your Personal Heart and calm your mind. It involves learning how to become more present in the moment. This reduces the time you spend in past or future thoughts. Meditation also opens your Personal Heart to create a stronger connection to your calm mind.

If you already have a meditation practice, then continue with it. But if you don't, there are many sources available to help you determine what works best for you. Some meditation resources offer guided or timed methods, while others focus on specific techniques, such as your breathing or a particular sound.

Explore these different meditation practices with an open mind and curiosity until you find one or two that you feel work best for you. Be open-hearted and mindful, and keep it simple. The most important factor here is not time, but consistency and having a routine. This takes practice. Be patient with yourself as you learn to open your Personal Heart and calm your mind to shift into the Mode of Love.

Just five minutes of meditation a day can enhance your mental clarity, calm your mind, and open your Personal Heart. Meditating first thing in the morning is a common time to practice calming your mind and opening your Personal Heart in the Mode of Love, so you can begin your day being more present and open-hearted. Also, meditating before bedtime may calm your mind, allowing you to fall asleep quickly and more deeply. If the meditation session is beneficial, offer gratitude for the experience. If you still feel overwhelmed with thoughts or feelings, try the Shift Tool in Chapter 20 for thoughts on a specific, stressful situation. Use the Reassurance Tool in Chapter 19 when you are overwhelmed, as another tool you can use to calm the mind.

Example of a Written Meditation

Let's go to Unconditional Love together. Read the next few paragraphs in a quiet place to experience the meditation:

Imagine being in your dream home. Find your favorite chair or sofa looking out at your favorite view. Now wrap yourself in a comfortable blanket. This blanket protects you from the outside world: the stress, responsibilities, and burdens. This blanket keeps outside stressors at bay.

You are now ready to focus on your breath. Imagine breathing in loving energy directly into your Personal Heart. With each slow, deep breath, you feel calmer. You feel yourself relaxing into the safety of the nurturing blanket. You feel safe and relaxed at this moment.

If you have any pain or discomfort, imagine that you can let go of it as you focus on loving energy with each breath. As you exhale, release any thoughts about the past or future, any frustrations occupying your mind, anything else distracting you from experiencing the flow of Unconditional Love.

As you experience this flow of Unconditional Love coming into your Personal Heart, begin to recognize the loving flow going out from your Personal Heart to every cell of your body. Feel this flow of love like gentle waves rolling calmly and magically into each cell. This is healing Unconditional Love connecting at the deepest cellular level. Imagine less pain here. Feel compassion and Unconditional Love for yourself in this moment. Continue to feel this flow of Unconditional Love the best you can until you are ready to return to the outside world.

When you are ready, gently wiggle your toes, wiggle your fingers, and slowly continue your day.

Sit in the calm of this meditation, as time allows, so you can thoroughly enjoy the flow of feeling love.

The Soul Moments Tool

Soul Moments are moments in the day where you feel your Personal Heart opening with Unconditional Love or compassion for yourself, others, animals, and nature. Soul moments can shift your Personal Heart into the Mode of Love because of the conscious awareness of Unconditional Love in that moment. Some examples are:

You suddenly feel connected to nature as you walk in the forest or on a beach.

You have overwhelming feelings of love for a partner, child, or friend.

You experience awe at the beauty of a sunset or sunrise.

You feel lots of love just being with others, watching children play, petting your cat or dog, having synchronistic moments, etc.

Be open to Soul Moments each day and allow your Personal Heart to open with Unconditional Love. Consciously experience and recognize these soul moments in your daily life and record them in your journal to remind yourself when it is not so easy to remember.

Practice

In the evening, get your journal and record any Soul Moments you experienced that day. Try to recognize how they made you feel. Did they change your thoughts, feelings, or behaviors? This tool helps you redirect your focus to recognize that Soul Moments are one way to connect you to more Unconditional Love in your daily experiences. This practice allows you to focus on what is feeling good in your life versus what is feeling stressful in your life. It enables you to recognize more loving experiences in your life and have a greater appreciation for these moments.

If this is a challenging exercise, you are most likely in the Mode of Fear. Practicing a tool to guide you to shift to the Mode of Love may be more beneficial. Begin with the Shift Tool in Chapter 20. Discovering more Soul Moments allows your Personal Heart to expand in the energy of love.

The Higher Vibrational Affirmation Tool

The purpose of the Higher Vibrational Affirmation Tool is to find a couple of higher vibrational statements that can assist you in strengthening a calm mind and opening your Personal Heart. Often, in stressful situations, we feel a pull toward fearful and judgmental thoughts. This tool allows you to transition from fear and judgment to thoughts of love that are supportive and encouraging.

Practice

Choose an affirmation or two from the following list of higher vibrational statements, or create your own, to support you in this moment. Not all statements will resonate with you in the same moment.

Mentally or verbally rehearse these higher vibrational affirmations, as many times as you need, to replace the lower vibrational thoughts. Use these higher vibrational statements to calm the mind quickly and to open your Personal Heart to prevent you from staying in lower vibrational thoughts in the moment.

- *I am safe* (only if this is true).
- *I can create safety for myself.*
- *I am lovable no matter what.*
- *I am good enough as I am.*
- *I have enough.*
- *Judging myself does not help me.*

- *Being kind to myself helps me.*
- *It is OK to make mistakes.*
- *I am loveable.*
- *I can calm my mind and open my Personal Heart.*
- *I love my Personal Heart Power.*
- *Remember, I am loved.*

You can find many additional higher vibrational statements online and in books. Find the statements that best support you to calm your mind and open your Personal Heart.

When the Higher Vibrational Affirmation Tool is not effective, try other tools or other higher vibrational practices such as:

- dancing,
- listening to music,
- reading,
- writing,
- journaling,
- creative activities,
- nature walks,
- laughing,
- joining and attending a group that inspires you,
- loving interactions with others.

The Heart Hugs Tool

The purpose of the Heart Hugs Tool is to practice the Personal Heart Taking and Giving Functions with Unconditional Love. The most precious gift you can give yourself in any present moment is Unconditional Love. Another precious gift in any present moment is giving Unconditional Love to others.

Practice

1. Close your eyes.
2. Place your hands on your heart or around your shoulders.
3. Take a deep breath into your Personal Heart.
4. Fully release the breath.
5. As you inhale again, imagine breathing in loving energy for yourself through your Personal Heart.
6. As you exhale, imagine sending loving energy to family, friends, or any living being.

Repeat this breathing pattern until you feel a sense of loving connection to yourself and others. You might feel your body relax and your mind calm down as you take each breath. Have fun giving yourself heart hugs in a variety of settings, like in your home, in a park, at work, in your parked car, or wherever you need a little more love for yourself. The more you give yourself heart hugs, the more likely giving out and taking in love will become a natural part of your day. Giving yourself as many heart hugs as you need each day is a loving way to connect with yourself in the present moment.

CHAPTER 19

Tool for the Disconnected Personal Heart State

This chapter focuses on the Disconnected Personal Heart Tool. There is just one tool in this chapter because using any tool is challenging when the mind is overwhelmed with chaos or completely shut down. The intention of this tool is to help reassure yourself so you can reduce the lower vibrational thoughts and feelings instead of overreacting, numbing, or avoiding them. Be kind to yourself the best you can. You are dealing with an abundant amount of overwhelming lower vibrational energies.

When you find yourself in the Disconnected Personal Heart State, please remember the Disconnected Personal Heart State is very challenging. You have taken a big step to search for tools to help you shift into a higher vibrational state. Remember to be kind to yourself in this Disconnected Personal Heart State; self-judging doesn't help or improve your Personal Heart State. In this stressful state, you often forget you have tools.

Ideally, seek additional external support as you begin your transition from the Disconnected Personal Heart State. When you are on your own, the following tool may support you in the moment.

The initial step to getting out of this Disconnected Personal Heart State is to become aware you are in it in the first place. Once you have this awareness, try the Reassurance Tool. This aims to reassure the mind and Personal Heart by reducing the effects of stress on the mind, heart, and body. Hopefully, it will help you shift out of the Disconnected Personal Heart State.

The Reassurance Tool

The Reassurance Tool has three components to assist you in connecting to a calmer mind:

- slower and deeper breathing techniques,
- verbal reassurance,
- and physical reassurance.

Remember, a calmer mind allows for the connection to your Personal Heart. Choose which components work most effectively to reassure you in the moment. Slower and deeper breathing allows you to calm the sympathetic nervous system. Typically, it needs to occur before you can effectively use the verbal and physical reassuring practices.

Verbally reassuring yourself will calm your stressed mind. Repeat the verbal reassurance over and over until you feel the lower vibrational thoughts subsiding in your mind. Physically reassuring yourself with a caring touch can also calm the body and mind. This tool is a way to reduce overwhelming thoughts and feelings.

Breathing Reassurance Practice

1. Breathe in through your nose, slowly and deeply, into your lower abdomen for the count of five seconds.

2. Breathe out slowly, from your nose or mouth, for the count of five seconds.

3. Repeat these steps until you feel your body relax physically and your mind calms down.

4. The number of breaths needed will depend upon how activated your sympathetic nervous system is in the moment. It is common for distracting thoughts to interrupt your focus on your breathing in this state. Be kind to yourself when they do, and try to refocus on your breath until you feel calmer.

Verbal Reassurance Practice

Use the most nurturing voice you can muster in this stressful moment and say to yourself one or two of the following simple statements. Choose the ones that feel reassuring to you in the moment.

Say the statements in a slow and steady rhythm to deactivate the sympathetic nervous system, which calms your mind and Personal Heart.

Say one or two statements slowly, out loud or in your head, until you feel calmer:

- *I am safe* (only if it is true in the moment).
- *I am good enough.*
- *I will not take this situation personally.*
- *I can let this go.*
- *I will get through this.*
- *At this moment, I am just a person* [doing an action]… (e.g. sitting, standing, walking).

Physical Reassurance Practice

For physical reassurance, choose one or more of these:

- Give yourself a big hug.
- Stroke your upper arms.
- Place your hands over your physical heart.

This practice serves to reassure and reconnect you with yourself physically in a healthy and safe way.

Explore each of these three practices until you discover the optimal combination for you to connect to a calmer mind and higher vibrational energies to shift into another Personal Heart State. Remember not to judge yourself for getting into a Disconnected Personal Heart State.

The more you practice this tool in the Disconnected Personal Heart State, the easier it is to connect to higher vibrational energies and shift into another Personal Heart State. Once you sense the relief from the overwhelming stress, you can then use the other Personal Heart Power Tools as needed.

CHAPTER 20

Tool for the Reactive Personal Heart State

In the Reactive Personal Heart State, you have a reactive heart and mind. Your Personal Heart is inclined to overreact to internal thoughts and external situations. Your mind is typically stuck in past or future thoughts. These stuck thoughts can lead to being trapped in a Stress Loop with stressful beliefs activated.

Stressful beliefs take you out of balance and into lower vibrational thoughts and feelings, which often lead to lower vibrational behaviors. Noticing these Stress Loops and their stressful beliefs allows you to make different and healthier choices—choices to support your shift to a higher vibrational Personal Heart State. For more intentional and longer-lasting effects, the Shift Tool may support your shift from this state to a higher vibrational Personal Heart State.

The Shift Tool

Use the Shift Tool when a stressful belief has been triggered by lower vibrational thoughts, feelings, or behaviors due to a *specific* stressful situation, a person, or a group of people. Once you know you are in the Reactive Personal Heart State, practice this tool.

Awareness allows you to choose which stressful belief you want to shift into a reassuring belief. This tool will help you become consciously aware of your triggered stressful belief within your Stress Loop. A reminder: a Stress Loop is when the mind is ruminating in past or future thoughts anchored by a certain stressful belief. A Stressful Belief is a belief that supports a lower vibrational belief system.

You can begin shifting your stressful belief by choosing a reassuring statement that restores your calm mind and opens your Personal Heart. Over time, repeating the reassuring statement encourages the transformation from a stressful belief to a reassuring belief. The intention is to catch Stress Loops as they become activated and then deactivate them more quickly to keep a calm mind and your Personal Heart operating from the Mode of Love.

The next table gives some examples of common stressful beliefs, their corresponding Stress Loops, and reassuring statements to shift out of the Stress Loops. You may have other Stress Loops with their own stressful beliefs you can add to this table. Determining a reassuring statement to shift yourself out of your Stress Loops is the desired outcome.

The Stressful Belief Chart

Stressful Belief	Stress Loop	Reassuring Statement
I am not good enough.	Not Good Enough Loop	I am good enough.
I am not loveable.	Not Loveable Loop	I am loveable.
It's my job to rescue others.	Rescuer Loop	It's not my job to rescue others.
It's my job to make other people happy.	People-pleasing Loop	It's not my job to make other people happy.
It's my job to fix people and things.	Fix-it Loop	It's not my job to fix people and things.
Other people should take care of me.	Victim Loop	I can take care of myself.
If I judge myself and others, it will help.	Judging Loop	Judging myself or others does not help.
I should be perfect.	Perfection Loop	I do not need to be perfect.
If I can control things, I will be safe.	Control Loop	I do not need to control things to be safe.
I can't trust anyone.	Can't Trust Loop	I can trust myself and others who are in balance.

The Shift Tool is best done when you are alone or with someone with whom you feel safe, who won't judge you, and with whom you can trust your feelings. This person can be a loving presence for you as you process through your feelings and shift out of the Stress Loop into a reassuring belief to restore the calm mind and open Personal Heart. Remember, it is not their job to rescue you from your feelings or situation, but to be a loving presence.

Practice

Summarize your one specific stressful situation in a few sentences. Considering multiple situations will take you off track.

Either say the story out loud or write it down in your journal.

My stressful situation is…

Sense from your Personal Heart what lower vibrational feelings arise regarding this specific situation.

The Lower Vibrations Feeling Chart

Afraid
Angry
Anxious
Depressed
Disappointed
Guilty
Helpless
Lonely
Overwhelmed
Sad
Stressed
Unlovable

The diagram lists the most common lower vibrational feelings. You may have other feelings that are not included here. It is important to process through all of your lower vibrational feelings, one at a time, as they relate to your specific stressful situation.

Use the *I feel…* statement until you have identified all your lower vibrational feelings in relation to this stressful situation.

I feel (lower vibrational feeling) because…

Keep the feeling statements limited to a short sentence to avoid going back into overthinking mode. Process through your feelings until the feeling of disappointment arises. Disappointment is the lower vibrational feeling that is triggered when you believe something should have happened but didn't, or something shouldn't have happened and it did.

As you state, *I feel…*, deeply and slowly inhale and exhale to support the processing through each lower vibrational feeling to release the energy each feeling holds.

With each breath cycle, try to feel the identified feeling the best you can within your body. This breathing technique allows the lower vibrational feeling to wane because you are consciously processing through the feelings. In consciousness, the body wants to release these lower vibrational feelings to rebalance. Movement of the body area can also support the release of the stuck energy. Remember, your body holds on to your lower vibrational feelings energetically because you have not processed through the lower vibrational feelings.

With this feeling-processing technique, you are allowing your body to release the lower vibrational feelings in a healthy way. When you begin to feel disappointment, you are ready to discover your stressful belief.

Identify and feel the disappointment. This disappointment feeling leads to what you think should have happened or should not have happened, which is usually the stressful belief.

I feel disappointed that...

Of course, I feel disappointed because my stressful belief is...

Once you have found the primary stressful belief, you are ready to shift to the higher vibrational thought: the reassuring belief. Choose a reassuring statement to support your shift into a reassuring belief supported by the Mode of Love.

I now choose to shift to a new reassuring statement, which is...

Repeat your reassuring statement while practicing the slow and deep breathing technique until your mind has calmed down enough to let go of the stressful belief. *You can't believe in both the stressful belief and the corresponding reassuring belief at the same time.* Saying the reassuring statement over and over until your mind calms down and the physical body relaxes helps to shift from the Mode of Fear to the Mode of Love, thus transforming from the stressful belief to the reassuring belief. Initially, it is common for the mind to resist the reassuring statement. It can take time for the shift to occur, from letting go of a stressful belief to believing the reassuring belief.

The transition occurs when the mind and body can relax into the present moment and start believing the reassuring statement. The transformation occurs when the reassuring statement becomes a reassuring belief. This tool supports more connection between your calm mind and Personal Heart. If, after practicing this tool, you remain stuck in any of the lower vibrational thoughts and feelings—

especially anger—try the Reassurance Tool in Chapter 19. Be patient and compassionate with yourself, the best you can, when you are in the Reactive Personal Heart State.

Quick Reference of Shift Tool Statements

My stressful situation is…

I feel (lower vibrational feeling) because… (for each feeling that rises)

I feel disappointed that…

Of course, I feel disappointed because my stressful belief is…

I now choose to shift to a new reassuring statement, which is…

Example of Using the Shift Tool

Consider the flowers example earlier in the book when we forgot to plant them and they died. This scenario can be a stressful situation that triggers stressful beliefs. The next example processes through this stressful situation using the Shift Tool:

My stressful story is: *I was so stupid. I left those beautiful flowers in the blazing sun to die.*

I feel angry because I didn't remember to plant the flowers.

Practice the deep breathing process to release this feeling of anger wherever you perceive it in your body. Once a feeling is released, note to see if another feeling arises. Process through each one as they arise. If releasing a feeling takes more than ten breath cycles, switch to the Reassurance Tool.

Now, back to the example:

I feel stupid because I didn't remember the flowers.

Practice the deep breathing process to release this feeling of feeling stupid wherever you perceive it in your body. Remember, movement of the body can be beneficial too.

I feel guilty because the flowers died.

Practice the deep breathing process to release this feeling of guilt wherever you perceive it in your body.

I feel sad because I will not be able to enjoy the flowers.

Practice the deep breathing process to release the feeling of sadness wherever you perceive it in your body.

I feel worried that I will kill new flowers if I buy more.

Practice the deep breathing process to release this feeling of worry wherever you perceive it in your body.

I feel disappointed that I wasn't perfect because I forgot about the flowers.

Of course, I feel disappointed because my stressful belief is…

Examples of stressful beliefs for this stressful situation:

- I should be perfect.
- I'm not good enough.

- I am bad for making a mistake.
- I can't do anything right.

Now choose to shift to a reassuring statement. Examples of reassuring statements for this stressful situation include:

- I do not need to be perfect to be wonderful.
- I am good enough.
- It's OK to make a mistake.
- I can do many things right.

As you repeat the reassuring statement out loud, silently in your head, or write it in your journal, practice the deep breathing process. Throughout the day and the following days, if the stressful story returns to your thoughts, remind yourself of the reassuring statement. The stressful belief wanes when your mind believes the reassuring statement to be true.

In the reactive heart, sometimes the Shift Tool can feel overwhelming. Other potential beneficial practices for the Reactive Personal Heart State include:

- connect with a supportive friend or family member,
- go for a walk,
- e-mail, text, or find a support group,
- seek professional support,
- healthy self-soothing,
- reading,
- listening to relaxing music,
- The Heart Hugs Tool, Chapter 18,
- short mantras,
- movement/exercise,

- time with loved ones,
- receive body or energy work,
- time in nature.

In a Reactive Personal Heart State, finding these healthy activities can be challenging to start with. This is an ongoing practice to discover what works best for your mind and Personal Heart in this state.

This Personal Heart State occurs when life gets stressful. Having tools to shift more quickly back to a calm mind and open Personal Heart eases the activation of Stress Loops. You show courage as you take conscious steps to find what works for enhancing your calm mind and connecting to your Personal Heart Power!

CHAPTER 21

Tools for the Half-Hearted Personal Heart State

In the Half-hearted Personal Heart State, you operate back and forth between the Mode of Fear and the Mode of Love. Shifting between these modes means you are more likely to have a wider vibrational range of thoughts, feelings, and behaviors. With awareness, you are more likely to sense when you are going out of balance. This awareness of imbalance allows you to choose to use tools to return to balance, stabilizing your operation from the Mode of Love.

When in the Mode of Fear, these tools will assist you in shifting into the Mode of Love more easily than in the previous states because you are closer to transitioning into the Mode of Love. When you're in the Mode of Love, using these tools will create more emotional resilience and balance on all levels as you transition closer to the Content Personal Heart State.

As with all states, the Personal Heart Assessment Tool of Chapter 14 provides the most detailed assessment of your Personal Heart. Using the assessment with the tools in Chapters 15, 16, and 17 will provide the most comprehensive support and balancing for this state.

The tools in this chapter provide practices that allow for a quicker vibrational shift into the Mode of Love in the moment.

The Gratitude Moments Tool

The Gratitude Moments Tool aims to connect you to the feeling of gratitude so you can remain in or shift to the Mode of Love. When you find yourself with that *glass-half-empty* mindset, where you are focusing on what you do not have instead of what you do have, gratitude can quickly help shift you out of the Mode of Fear. This tool can quickly remind you that life offers more abundance than you are remembering.

Examples of Gratitude Moments include feeling appreciation for someone loving you; appreciating a certain situation; feeling grateful for your health, life, friends, family members, work, and abundance in your life. Eventually, you may even find gratitude for the challenging moments you have experienced because of what you learned from the experience. This is when you realize life is happening *for* you. Keeping a daily gratitude journal reinforces and enhances this practice.

Practice

Grab your journal or recording device.

1. Intentionally pause for a moment, or some length of time, to consider what you can be grateful for. These can be moments, experiences, situations, people, or circumstances of your life from the past, present, or future.
2. As each thought rises, record it in your journal.
3. For each thought recorded, express your gratitude by incorporating any thoughts, feelings, and behaviors that would support your gratitude experience. Forms of gratitude may

be expressed as a simple thought of gratitude, feeling the appreciation, or expressing it through appreciative behaviors.

4. Incorporating gratitude moments throughout your day will assist you in living a love-focused life more consistently.

The Compassion Moments Tool

The Compassion Moments Tool is a practice to help you shift from judgment to compassion for yourself and others. Where compassion leads to connection, judgment leads to separation. This tool is a practice of creating ***Compassion Moments, which are moments of choosing compassion instead of judgment**. Compassion offers presence, understanding, and kindness to yourself or others in a stressful situation. When it is challenging for you to feel compassion, this becomes an opportunity to practice this tool consciously.

Practice

Become aware when you are judging a person or situation, including yourself. These are opportunities to shift from judgment to a Compassion Moment. This happens when you interrupt the judging thought by stopping it. The thought is stopped by re-centering your mind into the present moment and focusing on opening your Personal Heart in the Mode of Love. Focusing on the Personal Heart interrupts the judgment and allows compassion to flow more freely. This will allow you to become a loving presence for yourself and others in the stressful situation. You then operate from your Personal Heart Power.

Here are some examples of opportunities to practice compassion:

*   When someone is sharing a stressful story, you can be a listening and loving presence rather than sharing your story or judging their story.
*   When you or others make mistakes, poor choices, or do not meet certain expectations, you can offer empathy and learn from the situation.

- When it has been a challenging day with difficult choices that were painful or exhausting, use love and self-care to offer compassion for what you have been through.
- When you are feeling the essential pain of a situation, offer yourself or others compassion as you process through the lower vibrational feelings.

Reminder: compassion can only be given out or taken in when you have some ability to operate from your Personal Heart Power.

The Balancing Behaviors Tool

The Balancing Behaviors Tool helps you consciously choose higher vibrational behaviors to replace lower vibrational behaviors to function in the Mode of Love. This happens at a Choice Point.

Practice

Journaling allows you to see progress as you choose more higher vibrational behaviors.

Make a list of your lower vibrational behaviors. These are the behaviors that deplete your energy, vitality, sense of well-being, and interfere with your personal relationships.

For each behavior, think of some higher vibrational behaviors that you can use to replace the lower vibrational behaviors that will increase your energy, create a sense of wellbeing, and improve your personal relationships. If this is challenging, ask others who are supportive for ideas.

Make the choice to implement these higher vibrational behaviors. To implement your choice: make a manageable plan, create a support system, know the series of steps necessary for change, and celebrate little successes along the way.

For inspiration of higher vibrational behaviors, review the following list for general ideas.

The Vibrational Behavior Chart

Lower vibrational behaviors	Higher vibrational behaviors
sedentary lifestyle	more active lifestyle
addictive behavior	Seek supportive services or programs
poor sleeping habits	create a healthy sleep routine
eating non-nutritional food	eat more nutritional food
stressful relationships	set healthy boundaries with others
undesired job	seek a heart-inspired job

With the practice of shifting from lower vibrational behaviors into higher vibrational behaviors, you will feel higher vibrational thoughts and feelings, such as love, joy, and peace.

The Forgiveness Tool

The intention of The Forgiveness Tool is to forgive yourself and others. The opportunities to forgive can range from small things to seemingly unforgivable ones. When beginning this practice, start with the less challenging grievances towards yourself and others. As you use this practice, you will realize how forgiving increases your Personal Heart Power.

Practice

The release of grievances allows you to restore your calm mind and open your Personal Heart. Forgiveness releases you from the Stressful Beliefs of the past. Forgiveness does not mean the situation was acceptable. It simply means you no longer wish to hold on to the Stressful Belief that something in the past should have been different and you want to change it.

Find a safe place, allow some time, and bring your journal.

Think of one thing you need to forgive yourself or someone else for. Remember to begin with easier grievances and work up to the more challenging ones in your forgiveness practice. Success with forgiving the easier grievances will build your courage and desire to forgive the more challenging ones.

Ask yourself, *What am I getting out of holding onto this grievance?* Next, ask yourself, *Is this pain or frustration beneficial for me to hold on to?* You're at a Choice Point here: choosing not to forgive and holding onto grievances is being fueled by the Mode of Fear. Choosing to forgive is being fueled by the Mode of Love.

When you choose not to forgive, you can still help the forgiving process move forward by bringing up the lower vibrational feelings of the grievance and processing through them for your benefit to release the feelings.

When offering forgiveness to someone, it is more likely to be received if that person has a degree of an open Personal Heart for this situation. This is important to remember as you determine your method of forgiveness. Even if the other person cannot give or take in forgiveness, you can still do a practice to ease the pain and frustration for yourself. Some options for offering forgiveness include:

- energetically offering forgiveness to yourself or others through means such as prayer, meditation, journaling, or setting an intention for forgiveness,

- verbally expressing forgiveness to yourself or others when it feels safe,
- sending a letter, card, text, email, a phone call, or any way of expressing your forgiveness,
- seeking external support to process through a painful situation to forgive yourself or others.

Forgiveness is offered without attachment to the outcome. The reward of forgiveness is the release of your grievance's Stressful Belief, which helps you to restore a calm mind and open Personal Heart.

The Soul Eyes Tool

The Soul Eyes Tool exists to assist you in looking at yourself with filters of Unconditional Love rather than filters of judgment. *The eyes are the window to the soul,* is a common phrase. What is the window of your eyes seeing? The soul eyes see you and the world as beautiful and amazing. The judging eyes see everything that is wrong with you and the world.

The Soul Eyes tool takes this a step further and creates your own soul eyes: how you look at yourself and the world with love instead of judgment. It takes practice to see with soul eyes. As you see with your soul eyes, your Personal Heart Power is engaged.

Practice

1. As you begin, set a timer for two minutes.
2. Stand in front of a mirror. Close your eyes and take a slow, deep breath in, and as you exhale, let go of any judging filters you might have. Practice replacing the judging filter with the loving filter.
3. Now open your eyes and look in the mirror, seeing all of yourself with love and compassion. Be kind because this is often a challenge.

4. When judging thoughts arise, shift your thoughts to a reassuring belief and repeat it until the judgment wanes.

5. Now, imagine your soul eyes can see you with compassion and Unconditional Love. Your soul eyes cannot recognize the imperfections your judge notices. They recognize you as a loveable person.

6. After two minutes, notice how you are looking at yourself with your soul eyes and how that makes you think and feel.

7. Record the experience of this process so you can look back and recognize progress in the future.

Appreciate any loving experiences as you see your authentic self. Your new awareness allows you to make choices to live from a soul eyes perspective more often. This is operating from your Personal Heart Power.

CHAPTER 22

Tools for the Content Personal Heart State

In the Content Personal Heart State, your Personal Heart is primarily filled with higher vibrational energy, and you feel content. This contentment allows your heart to flow in love more easily in your life. The primary focus in this state is to strengthen the connection between your open Personal Heart and calm mind in relation to Unconditional Love: your Personal Heart Power.

The Content Personal Heart State is about remaining in optimal balance by continuing to use the tools that have been working for you to increase your Personal Heart Power. It's this wonderful feeling of contentment that becomes the motivator to remain in this state. The following tools will support you in all aspects of your Personal Heart and your ability to operate in the Mode of Love.

The Love Moments Tool
The Love Moments Tool is about intentionally pausing to sense and feel love. It is also about feeling and offering gratitude for experiencing love.

Doing this allows your Personal Heart to remain open and maintain a love-focused life. Recognizing the love around you will support you in maintaining and continually expanding your Personal Heart. Journaling about your love moments can be beneficial so you can return to them when you need reminders of loving moments.

Practice

1. Complete any of the following statements that are supportive of your Content Personal Heart State:

    *   In this moment I feel love for...
    *   I feel love when...
    *   I can create a loving moment by...
    *   I experience sharing love with...
    *   Love surprised me when...
    *   I love to...

2. Allow your Personal Heart to take in fully the magnitude of the loving memories from these statements.
3. Offer gratitude for the loving experiences.
4. Create a daily routine where you look for and appreciate Love moments.

This practice sets the intention for a love-focused day.

The Connection Tool

The purpose of the Connection Tool is to reinforce intentionally the connection between the open Personal Heart and the calm mind. When you feel this connection weakening, this tool becomes a gentle practice for you to realign or reinforce your connection between your Personal Heart and the calm mind.

Practice

1. Sit quietly and pause for several minutes.
2. Imagine a continuous reciprocal connection between your open Personal Heart and your calm mind. This reciprocal connection could be imagined as a figure-of-eight loop, a circle, a spiral, or whatever image comes to you.
3. With this connection, repeat, "Unconditional Love flows easily between my Personal Heart and calm mind."
4. Repeat this until you feel the flow of a love-focused connection between the Personal Heart and calm mind.
5. Enjoy the higher vibrational feelings of this practice. This can be practiced anywhere, at any moment, to maintain a loving connection.

Other supportive tools to strengthen the Content Personal Heart State include any Personal Heart Power Tools, affirmations, gratitude journal, prayer, meditation, acts of kindness, or any other practice that maintains a calm mind and open Personal Heart.

CHAPTER 23

Tools for the Whole
Personal Heart State

The Tools for the Whole Personal Heart State are about operating from your Personal Heart Power. You are fully aware of your connection and operation with the Source of Unconditional Love and you intend to preserve it.

The Whole Heart Tool

The Whole Heart Tool helps you consciously activate or maintain your Whole Personal Heart State. This occurs when you can keep your Personal Heart open to take in and give out Unconditional Love freely. There are three key phrases you will focus on to open and expand your Personal Heart to connect with the Source of Unconditional Love:

1. *I am Lovable* – this phrase activates the Personal Heart *Taking* Function and helps you take in Unconditional Love into your Personal Heart.

2. *I am Loving* - this phrase activates the Personal Heart *Giving* Function and helps you give out Unconditional Love to others.

3. *I am Love* - this phrase activates the connection with the Source of Unconditional Love. With this statement, there is no separation from the Source of Unconditional Love.

Practice

1. Find a quiet place to sit or lie down.

2. Going in sequence, say out loud the first phrase, "I am loveable," until you consciously feel you are taking in Unconditional Love.

3. Continue with the second phrase by saying out loud, "I am loving," until you consciously feel you are giving out Unconditional Love.

4. Continue with the third phrase by saying out loud, "I am Love," until you consciously feel oneness to Unconditional Love.

5. Now say all three phrases several times in sequence until you feel the flow of Unconditional Love for yourself and others.

This tool enhances the connection with the Source of Unconditional Love because you are activating or maintaining the Whole Personal Heart State. Ultimately, you want to feel a oneness with the Source of Unconditional Love. Spend time in the silence appreciating this loving connection. Practice this tool regularly to support your Whole Personal Heart State.

The Unconditional Love Beacon Tool

An Unconditional Love Beacon is when you radiate Unconditional Love in the moment, wherever you may be. This is not about *doing* something; it is about you *being* something. It is being the presence of Unconditional Love—an Unconditional Love beacon. The Unconditional Love Beacon Tool helps you radiate love out to others.

Practice

1. Set the intention to be fully present with your open Personal Heart and calm mind.

2. Allow your loving higher vibrational energy to radiate out to others just by being a loving presence. Your ability to become a beacon of love can inspire others to become a beacon of love, too.

3. Be aware that sometimes when others are in one of the lower vibrational Personal Heart States, they may not be able to take in the fullness of your bright, loving light. It is a loving gesture to adjust the amount of love you share so you do not overwhelm people who are in lower vibrational Personal Heart States.

4. Have fun radiating your love and being an Unconditional Love beacon in the world!

Use any tools from your Personal Heart Toolbox to maintain the flow of Unconditional Love into and out of your Personal Heart. This Whole Personal Heart State focuses on awareness of the abundance of Unconditional Love to support you in everything that occurs in your life. This is the ultimate Personal Heart Power!

Practice these tools to remain in the Whole Personal Heart State more frequently and for longer periods. Remember, it takes many higher vibrational thoughts, feelings, and behaviors to experience this Personal Heart State. It takes many more to maintain the Whole Personal Heart State.

Conclusion

Congratulations on following your commitment by courageously and persistently taking this Personal Heart journey and learning more about your Personal Heart Power! Hopefully, you have discovered more about your Personal Heart, your mind, and your relationship with the Source of Unconditional Love, and you're excited to continue your love-focused life using your Personal Heart Power!

Wherever you are in your Personal Heart Power journey, we hope you now have a clearer understanding of how awareness plays an important role in determining your Mode of Operation for your Personal Heart and mind. Conscious awareness allows you to make choices to live more often in the Mode of Love, where fear is your informant, rather than living in the Mode of Fear, where love is typically conditional. This understanding allows you to know the importance of your vibrational choices and how they play out in your life. The five Personal Heart States create a framework you can rely on to assist you in maintaining a reference point for how your Personal Heart is operating in any moment.

Assessing your four Personal Heart Chambers and four Personal Heart Pillars, with conscious awareness, provides insight into your Personal Heart balance. Celebrate where you are balanced. When you are not in balance, pull out your Personal Heart Power Toolbox and practice one or more of the tools. Practicing the different Personal Heart Tools gives you the ability to shift into higher vibrational thoughts, feelings, and behaviors to restore balance in your Personal Heart.

The four Personal Heart Functions provide a way to manage the vibrational energies within your Personal Heart. Operating from the Mode of Love in your heart functions allows for the higher vibrational energy to flow in your Personal Heart. Exploration and understanding of the Personal Heart Functions give you insight and the ability to operate with your Personal Heart Power.

Understanding the Personal Heart framework provides you with the foundation to develop a deeper connection with yourself, others, and the Source of Unconditional Love. You now know that each vibrational choice you make with your thoughts, feelings, and behaviors determines your Mode of Operation: Fear or Love. Each Choice Point has become an opportunity to move towards or away from your Personal Heart Power. Your conscious awareness of these choices allows you to have the power to create transitions toward transformation into your love-focused life.

Bringing this all together means that you can now know, influence, and determine your life's outcomes consciously, based on the vibrational quality of your thoughts, feelings, and behaviors. The Personal Heart Tools presented in this book, and other tools you may have accumulated throughout your life, have filled your Personal Heart Power Toolbox. These tools can support your Personal Heart and mind to manage vibrational energies effectively to maintain an open Personal Heart and calm mind. Effective use of these tools will allow you to operate from your Personal Heart Power more often.

Celebrate every step you have taken, every tool you have practiced, and every nugget of wisdom you have gained to be where you are now. Whichever Personal Heart State you are in right now is appropriate for you in this moment on your journey. Your joys, your discoveries, your insights, your awareness, your transitions, and your accomplishments allow you to recognize the benefits of connecting to your Personal Heart Power.

Realize that your challenges, your fears, your tears, your setbacks, and your temptation to quit are also a part of your Personal Heart Power journey. These challenges are important to embrace, without judgment, to connect fully to your Personal Heart Power. Having tools to handle the lower vibrational challenges effectively allows you to transform into higher vibrational experiences, including love, joy, and peace. The ability to shift from your lower to higher vibrational energies allows you to create your love-focused life. You can transition into a new way of functioning in your Personal Heart.

As you choose to transition to a higher vibrational Personal Heart State in your journey, ultimately, you will be led to transformation. Transformation leads you to be changed forever. When you do all the necessary work to transform and operate from the Mode of Love, you will enjoy your own inner dream home. When you transform to saying, "Yes," and to owning your inner dream home, you make your Personal Heart your home sweet home. For yourself, for others, and for the world, we thank you for being on your Personal Heart Power journey!

We Offer Gratitude

This Personal Heart Power book is built upon all the love, knowledge, and wisdom we have received through our educational degrees, certifications, workshops, retreats, life lessons, relationships, and the heart resonance field. Many voices have inspired this book to come to fruition. We have an overflowing appreciation for each of them!

The most influential is the Voice of the Source of Unconditional Love itself. This Voice taught and transformed us abundantly on our own journeys from Fear to Unconditional Love. It also provided many other voices of support to carry us through to the completion of this book, especially during the most challenging moments.

The first person we wish to acknowledge is Nina Patrick. Nina followed an impulse and brought the two of us together. Without her, it is difficult to imagine this book at all. A special shout out to our early readers who made this book better: Judith Hower, Kathy Waldman, Bill Pohlad, Heather McElhatton Nicora, Kelly Rogers-Winston, and Deb Sakry Lande. We are also grateful to Jennifer Greb for capturing our essence in her photos.

We offer a special, loving thanks to our many teachers, soul sisters, families, and friends. There are too many to name, but we hope you know who you are. We have felt your love, support, and encouragement deep in our Personal Hearts. We would be remiss if we did not recognize the loving support of writing in nature and appreciating Gaia—Mother Nature—for all the resources she offers. A pause for Barbara Marx Hubbard and Sr. Marcia Jehn, for their Unconditional Love and unstoppable faith as we journeyed together.

We especially would like to thank the Global Heart Team, Good of the Whole, and each person who holds the Heart Resonance Field for their loving support.

We feel incredible gratitude to Christine Kloser and her entire team at Capucia Publishing for bringing this book to fruition. Thank you, Carrie Jareed, Jean Merrill, Karen Everitt, and Penny Legg, for guiding us beautifully throughout the publishing phase, even in the most challenging moments. With the gift of editing, Simon Whaley rose to the challenge and definitely improved our book. We could not have completed this book without any one of you.

To our families of origin, who gave each of us the foundation of early life experiences that formed us into the women we are today, we love you and appreciate what you have brought into our lives. A special moment of compassion for both of our dads, Grace's mom, and her sister, who all passed on as we wrote this book. For our children who love us unconditionally and teach us lessons on how to be more loving mothers, we love all of you with our Personal Hearts wide open.

Last, but not least, to our husbands—Steve Greb and Bill Pohlad—for being our rocks (or should we say minerals) as they stepped up with extra support and encouragement during the creation of this book. Thank you both for being our beloved soul mates and for believing in us and our Personal Heart mission. We feel grateful for our Personal Heart Power expanding during the writing of this book. We look forward to what is yet to come.

With abundant gratitude, love, and blessings, we say thank you to each person who has been an inspiration to our Personal Heart Power journey!

Glossary

Choice Point: The moment when we are consciously aware we have a choice and then we make a conscious decision rather than a subconscious one.

Compassion Moments: Moments of choosing compassion instead of judgment.

Conditional Love: Love with prerequisites or expectations.

Conscious Awareness: Our ability to recognize the information we have in the present moment.

Content Personal Heart State: We operate primarily from the Mode of Love and we use fear as an informant. We primarily function with higher vibrational thoughts, feelings, and behaviors. The range of experience tends to be on a continuum from manageable to fulfilled, with the ability to remain present in the current moment more often.

Disconnected Personal Heart State: Feels completely disconnected from the Mode of Love and entirely connected to the Mode of Fear. The Personal Heart is operating from the lowest vibrational thoughts, feelings, and behaviors. The range of experiences is from numbness to extreme overwhelm.

Emotional Intelligence: Our awareness of our feelings combined with our effective processing of these feelings with our mind.

Energy: The vibrational frequency we operate from within our Personal Heart: Fear or Love.

Global Heart: The collective energy of the world's individual Personal Hearts.

Global Heart Power: When the world's collective Personal Hearts are in community and primarily functioning from their Personal Heart Power from the Mode of Love.

Half-hearted Personal Heart State: We shift freely between operating from the Mode of Fear and the Mode of Love in our Personal Heart, depending on our perception of the current situation. There is an ebb and flow between the lower and higher vibrational thoughts, feelings, and behaviors. The range of experience tends to be on a continuum, from less stressful to somewhat manageable, often swinging like a pendulum depending upon the perception of the situation.

Mode of Fear: The Personal Heart is operating primarily with lower vibrational energies.

Mode of Love: The Personal Heart is operating primarily with higher vibrational energies.

Mode of Operation: How we are managing the range of vibrational energy in our Personal Heart at any given time. This determines whether we are operating from the Mode of Fear or the Mode of Love.

Personal Heart: The sensory center for the collective energetic experiences of your thoughts, feelings, and behaviors in relation to the primary vibrational energies—the Mode of Fear and the Mode of Love.

Personal Heart Chamber: A particular aspect of the Personal Heart. There are four Personal Heart Chambers: Energetic, Physical, Sensing, and Spiritual. Each chamber has a unique function.

Personal Heart Community Pillar: Stabilizes our Personal Heart in relationship with others.

Personal Heart Dismissing Function: Prevents vibrational energies from coming into our Personal Heart.

Personal Heart Energetic Chamber: Contains the energetic continuum of the vibrational frequencies in the Mode of Fear and the Mode of Love, and how they interact through our thoughts, feelings, and behaviors energetically.

Personal Heart Functions: The way energy is managed within the Personal Heart. There are four Personal Heart Functions: Taking, Dismissing, Giving, and Withholding.

Personal Heart Giving Function: Sends vibrational energies out from the Personal Heart.

Personal Heart Physical Chamber: Relates to the physical status of the entire physical body and is affected by the Mode of Love and the Mode of Fear.

Personal Heart Pillars: The stabilizers of our Personal Heart. The four Personal Heart Pillars are Presence, Safety, Unconditional Love, and Community.

Personal Heart Power: The ability to operate from the Mode of Love within our Personal Heart while interacting optimally with a calm mind.

Personal Heart Power Tools: Specific practices for increasing your Personal Heart Power.

Personal Heart Presence Pillar: Determines our ability to be present in the current moment. Its strength depends upon how much we can focus on the current moment and how we can decrease distractions that pull us out of this moment.

Personal Heart Safety Pillar: Provides the sense of protection and well-being which is determined by our perception of any situation. The strength of this pillar is based on our thoughts, feelings, and behaviors from previous experiences, as well as our perception of the current situation. Our sense of safety varies from moment to moment and from situation to situation.

Personal Heart Sensing Chamber: Contains the sensing of feelings within our Personal Heart and sends feeling information to the mind. The Personal Heart Sensing Chamber is supported energetically by the Mode of Fear and Mode of Love.

Personal Heart Spiritual Chamber: Contains our perception, our ability, and the quality of our connection to the Source of Unconditional Love.

Personal Heart State: Reflects how our Personal Heart is operating in connection to the energies of fear and love. It is the qualities and quantities of the energies' vibrational frequencies within the Personal Heart that determine our Personal Heart State. There are five Personal Heart States: Disconnected, Reactive, Half-hearted, Content, and Whole.

Personal Heart Taking Function: Manages the quality and quantity of the vibrational energies we take into our Personal Heart.

Personal Heart Unconditional Love Pillar: Our connection to the Source of Unconditional Love. Connection to the Source gives us the ability to love ourselves and others unconditionally.

Personal Heart Withholding Function: Suppresses vibrational energies from being given out from the Personal Heart.

Reactive Personal Heart State: Operating mainly from lower vibrational thoughts, feelings, and behaviors, from the Mode of Fear. However, it is not completely disconnected from the Mode of Love. The range of experiences is from overwhelmed to stressful.

Reassuring Belief: A higher vibrational belief.

Reassuring Statement: A higher vibrational thought or statement used for transitioning into a calm mind.

Self-love: The ability to love yourself unconditionally.

Source of Unconditional Love: The origin of the energy that fuels our Personal Heart with Unconditional Love. This is the Source of Unconditional Love people have called God, Allah, Buddha, Source, The Universe, Gaia, and other names.

Stress Loop: When the mind is ruminating in thoughts about the past or future, which are anchored by a certain stressful belief.

Stressful Belief: A thought that carries lower vibrational energies and is incorporated into the belief system we operate from.

Transformation: A series of transitions that lead to the major shift from living life primarily from the Mode of Fear to living life primarily from the Mode of Love in our Personal Heart.

Transformational Sequence: A series of choices rooted in love that lead to greater Personal Heart Power.

Transition: A series of consistent choices rooted in higher vibrational thoughts, feelings, and behaviors.

Transition Point: The moment we allow a transitioning process to begin towards a new way of being.

Unconditional Love: Loving energy without expectations.

Vibrational Frequency: The range of energies we experience within our Personal Heart.

Whole Personal Heart State: We are operating from the Mode of Love and feeling connected with the Source of Unconditional Love. We function with higher vibrational thoughts, feelings, and behaviors. There is no range of experience. It is enlightenment: an experience of wholeness and oneness, where the illusion of separation from the Source of Unconditional Love and others no longer exists.

Notes

1. Echart Tolle. *The Power of Now.* (Yellow Kite, 2001)

2. Dr Daniel Siegel M.D., *Aware: The Science and Practice of Presence.* (TarcherPerigee, 2020)

3. Thich Nhat Hanh. *The Miracle of Mindfulness.* (Beacon Press, 1999)

4. Laurel Mellin, PhD. *Wired for Joy.* (Hay House, 2010)

5. Shirzad Chamine. *Positive Intelligence.* (Greenleaf Book Group, 2012)

6. Dr. David Hawkins. *Power vs Force.* (Hay House, 2014)

7. https://www.heartmath.org/science/

8. Wayne Dyer. *The Power of Intention* (Hay House, 2005)

9. Rhonda Byrne. *The Secret* (Atria Books/Beyond Words. 1996)

10. Lynne McTaggart. *The Power of Eight: Harnessing the Miraculous Energies of a Small Group to Heal Others, Your Life, and the World* (Atria Books, 2018)

11. William Arntz, Betsy Chasse, Mark Vincente. *What the Bleep Do We Know!?* (20th Century Fox, 2005)

12. David R. Hawkins, *Power vs. Force.* (Hay House, 2014)

13. David DiSalvo, *Your Brain Sees Even When You Don't*. (https://www.forbes.com/sites/daviddisalvo/2013/06/22/your-brain-sees-even-when-you-dont/)

14. Statista. "Percentage of the population in the United States who have completed high school or more from 1960 to 2020, by gender." Last modified April 2021. https://www.statista.com/statistics/184266/educational-attainment-of-high-school-diploma-or-higher-by-gender/

15. Statista. "Percentage of the U.S. population who have completed four years of college or more from 1940 to 2020, by gender." Last modified April 2021. https://www.statista.com/statistics/184272/educational-attainment-of-college-diploma-or-higher-by-gender/

16. Hubbard, *52 Codes for Conscious Self Evolution*, p58. http://www.newnaturalness.nu/wp-content/uploads/52Codes.pdf

17. Einstein, Albert. "The Collected Papers of Albert Einstein." 2014. https://einsteinpapers.press.princeton.edu/

18. Barbara Marx Hubbard, *The Evolutionary Testament of Co-creation*. Muse Harbor Publishing (2015)

Bibliography

Arntz, William, Betsy Chasse, and Mark Vincente. "What the Bleep Do We Know!?" Lord of the Wind Film, LLC. 2013. https://whatthebleep.com/

Byrne, Rhonda. *The Secret*. New York. Atria Books/Beyond Words. 1996.

DiSalvo, David. "Your Brain Sees Even When You Don't." *Forbes.com*, June 22, 2013. https://www.forbes.com/sites/daviddisalvo/2013/06/22/your-brain-sees-even-when-you-dont/?sh=51d7bb7b116a

Dyer, Wayne. *The Power of Intention*. Carlsbad: Hay House. 2005.

Einstein, Albert. "The Collected Papers of Albert Einstein." 2014. https://einsteinpapers.press.princeton.edu/

Good of the Whole, LLC. 2021. http://www.goodofthewhole.org.

Hawkins, David R. *Power vs. Force: The Hidden Determinants of Human Behavior*. Carlsbad: Hay House, Inc.

HeartMath Institute. 2021. https://www.heartmath.org/

Hubbard, Barbara Marx. *52 Codes for Conscious Self Evolution*. Santa Barbara: Foundation for Conscious Evolution, 2011.

Hubbard, Barbara Marx. *The Evolutionary Testament of Co-Creation*. Los Angeles: Muse Harbor Publishing, 2015.

McTaggart, Lynne. *The Power of Eight: Harnessing the Miraculous Energies of a Small Group to Heal Others, Your Life, and the World*. New York: Atria Paperback, 2018.

Mellin, Laurel. *Wired for Joy: A Revolutionary Method for Creating Happiness from Within*. Carlsbad: Hay House, 2010.

Dictionary.com. "Energy" 2022. https://www.dictionary.com/browse/energy

Dictionary.com. "Self-love." 2022. https://www.dictionary.com/browse/self-love

Dictionary.com. "Transformation." 2022. https://www.dictionary.com/browse/transformation

Statista. "Percentage of the U.S. population who have completed four years of college or more from 1940 to 2020, by gender." Last modified April 2021. https://www.statista.com/statistics/184272/educational-attainment-of-college-diploma-or-higher-by-gender/

Statista. "Percentage of the population in the United States who have completed high school or more from 1960 to 2020, by gender." Last modified April 2021. https://www.statista.com/statistics/184266/educational-attainment-of-high-school-diploma-or-higher-by-gender/

About the Authors

Grace Lynn

Grace Lynn, also known as Theresa Barry-Greb PT, MS, is the co-founder of the Global Heart Team and creator of the Loving Journey program.

Her path to becoming the co-author of *Personal Heart Power* and creator of the *Loving Journey Program* began by helping people as a licensed physical therapist with a Bachelor of Health Science in Physical Therapy from the University of Kentucky. During the thirty-six years of her physical therapy practice, she recognized the need for additional holistic services that support mental, emotional, energetic, and spiritual well-being in addition to physical healing. Her desire to teach others is enhanced by her Master of Science degree in  Education from the University of Kentucky and extensive certifications in a variety of complementary healing practices, including Enneagram, Psychosynthesis, Emotional Brain Training, Projective Dream Work, Breathwork, Intuitive Energy, and Reiki master. Grace's mission and commitment is to support people's transformational shift from struggling with their fear-based beliefs to embracing a love-focused life full of possibilities.

For over twenty years, Grace has been deeply devoted to helping people achieve a love-focused life through her coaching practice and facilitating many groups, including Loving Journey, Projective Dream Work, Global Heart Team, and Emotional Brain Training groups. She has also taught many workshops on various topics, including Loving Journey, Global Heart, Psychosynthesis, Projective Dream Work, Enneagram, Emotional Brain Training, Breathwork, and Energy work.

Grace is the co-founder of the Global Heart Team, whose mission is to stand in LOVE and collectively shift the fear-based humanity into a love-focused humanity. To learn more about Grace, the Loving Journey program, Global Heart Team, workshops, and retreats visit www.globalheartteam.org.

Michelle Marie

Michelle Marie is a dynamic transformational visionary who is most invigorated when guiding people to reach their fullest potential for a love-focused life.

Her formal education began with a Bachelor of Science degree at the University of Minnesota and continued with graduate certificates in Child Abuse Prevention, Agent of Conscious Evolution, Peace Ambassador, and Magdalene Rose Priestess Mastery Program. She was also mentored for one year by Barbara Marx Hubbard.

Her education, combined with decades of experience in management, philanthropy, training, facilitation, speaking, and program implementation, has allowed her to work in a variety of capacities. She has served on several prominent boards of directors, bolstering significant changes by utilizing her skill set of reaching for the greatest potential. Michelle has led initiatives for affordable housing, life-skills training, program development and implementation, and philanthropic events. She has volunteered in service to people, raised substantial amounts in funding, and used her voice for change. Her greatest achievements include a $21 million capital campaign for CommonBond Communities for affordable housing, shifting Ripple Effects Images from a start-up to a legacy organization to empower women and children, and creating her love-focused initiative to support others toward their love-focused life.

Michelle's circuitous journey eventually connected as she became a co-author of *Personal Heart Power* and creator of *Love Voice Rising*. She wants to do her part to transform our world into one that is rooted in love. She has built a unique skill set to guide people effectively to breakthroughs. Her ability to be insightful combines her lived experiences with listening, absorbing, honoring, and unfolding the stories others share with her for transforming toward a love-focused life. Many who have known her will say she has a way to peer into their souls and pull out their truth to help them see their best selves.

Currently, Michelle guides through private sessions with individuals who have varying needs, organizes and facilitates group programs, and leads retreats. To learn more, visit www.lovevoicerising.com.

Made in the USA
Middletown, DE
14 October 2022

12744010R00161